Roles and Performances in Apuleius' *Metamorphoses*

DRAMA

Beiträge zum antiken Drama
und seiner Rezeption

Herausgegeben von
F. De Martino – J. A. López Férez –
G. Mastromarco – B. Seidensticker –
N. W. Slater – A. H. Sommerstein –
R. Stillers – P. Thiercy –
B. Zimmermann

Stavros Frangoulidis

Roles an Performances in Apuleius' *Metamorphoses*

Verlag J. B. Metzler
Stuttgart · Weimar

Die Deutsche Bibliothek - CIP-Einheitsaufnahme

Frangoulidis, Stavros:
Roles and Performances in Apuleius' *Metamorphoses*/Stavros Frangoulidis.
- Stuttgart ; Weimar : Metzler, 2001
(Drama : Beiheft ; 16)
(M-&-P-Schriftenreihe für Wissenschaft und Forschung)

ISBN 978-3-476-45284-9
ISBN 978-3-476-02841-9 (eBook)
DOI 10.1007/978-3-476-02841-9

Dieses Werk einschließlich aller seiner Teile ist urheberrechtlich geschützt. Jede Verwertung außerhalb der engen Grenzen des Urheberrechtsgesetzes ist ohne Zustimmung des Verlages unzulässig und strafbar. Das gilt insbesondere für Vervielfältigungen, Übersetzungen, Mikroverfilmungen und die Einspeicherung und Verarbeitung in elektronischen Systemen.

M & P Schriftenreihe für Wissenschaft und Forschung
www.metzlerverlag.de
Info@metzlerverlag.de

© 2001 Springer-Verlag GmbH Germany
Ursprünglich erschienen bei J.B.Metzlersche Verlagsbuchhandlung
und Carl Ernst Poeschel Verlag GmbH in Stuttgart 2001

CONTENTS

Acknowledgements vii

Introduction 1

Chapter I - Unwittingly Successful Performances:
The Triumph of Magic 15
   1. From Friend to Unwitting Enemy: Aristomenes'
      Tale of Socrates 16
   2. Mutilation as Emasculation: Thelyphron's
      Tale of Thelyphron 35
   3. The Laughter festival as a Community Integration Rite 49

Chapter II - Fatally Successful Performances 69
   1. The New Recruit's Tale of Plotina 70
   2. A Faithful Wife's Revenge: The Servant's
      Tale of Charite 82

Chapter III - Unsuccessful Performances 105
   1. The Ass as Helper? The Ass' Tale of the Miller's Wife 105
   2. The Tale of the Stepmother as a Variant of
      Thelyphron's Tale 119

Chapter IV - Man and Animal 129
   1. 'Theater' and 'Spectacle:' The Robber's Tale
      of Thrasyleon 129
   2. Thiasos and Venus in the Corinthian Theater 147

Chapter V - Successful Performances:
Lucius' Spiritual Journey 163

Bibliography 177

General Index 191

ACKNOWLEDGEMENTS

This study offers an analysis of selected embedded tales and longer narrative sequences in Apuleius' *Metamorphoses* from the perspective of 'roles' and 'performances' as defined by the Greimasian discourse model. Chapters I.1, II.2, III.1 and IV.1 are revised versions of articles in *CJ* 95 (1999) 375-391, *AJP* 120 (1999) 601-619, *Scholia* 9 (2000) 66-78, and *Drama* 8 (1999) 113-135 respectively. I would like to thank the editors of these journals: Peter E. Knox, Philip A. Stadter, William J. Dominik and Bernhard Zimmermann for granting me permission to reuse those earlier works. The illustration of Isis Pelagia on the cover is from a fragmentary lamp found in Sarapieion C at Delos (Inv. No. B 2984, photo by ÉFA, E. Sérafis). I wish to thank the École française d'Athènes and its Director Prof. Roland Étienne for their permission to use the photograph. In this study, I do not examine the tale of Cupid and Psyche, which I have already discussed in the Appendix of my earlier monograph, *Handlung und Nebenhandlung: Theater, Metatheater und Gattungsbewusstsein in der römischen Komödie* (Stuttgart: Metzler 1997) 145-177.

Heartfelt thanks are due to S.N. Philippides for the extensive discussions, which originally inspired the theoretical approach of this work, and for his subsequent tireless encouragement. I would also like to thank several colleagues and friends who read versions of the book and made helpful comments: Yannis Tzifopoulos, S.N. Philippides, Michael Paschalis, John L. Penwill, David Konstan, David George, S.J. Harrison, Alfred Vincent, Sophia Papaioannou, Christos Tsagalis, Nic Panagopoulos and Ben Petre.

I also wish to express my thanks to those colleagues and friends who supplied me with copies of their work or with other relevant material: Maaike Zimmerman, Sophia Papaioannou, Maria Sarinaki and Dimitris Kritsotakis. Manolis Skountakis has carefully checked all the Latin quotations. I am grateful to Professor Dr. Bernhard Zimmermann, editor-in-charge, for the renewed opportunity to publish my work in the monograph series of *Drama*, as well as for his astute suggestions, his hospitality and his encouragement.

The text of Apuleius' *Metamorphoses* is quoted from Helm's Teubner edition (1992), unless otherwise indicated. All Latin translations of Apuleius are from Hanson's Loeb edition (1989).

Rethymno, April 2001

INTRODUCTION

Apuleius' *Metamorphoses* relates the story of Lucius' change into an ass through magic; his sorrowful adventures as he is sold to various masters and his travels through different communities; his restoration, both physically and spiritually, through Isis' help and, finally, his initiations into the rites of Isis and her brother/consort Osiris.

The narrative of the *Metamorphoses* incorporates various descriptions and sequences which refer to theatrical and dramatic performances. Several scholars have drawn attention to amphitheater performances and/or pantomimes. Niall W. Slater discusses various amphitheater performances in the novel and suggests that the notion of spectacle has negative connotations in the narrative.[1] On the other hand, Maaike Zimmerman focuses on theatrical aspects in the *ekphrasis* of the Judgment of Paris, the pantomime, in the final sequence of Lucius' asinine adventures before his restoration to human form (Book 10).[2]

The novel has not so far been assessed from the perspective of 'roles' and 'performances' on the discourse level.[3] Such a reading is warranted by the fact that most major characters in the novel constantly change roles. This behavior constitutes an important

---

[1] Slater 2000, 110-11.
[2] Zimmerman 1993.
[3] Winkler 1985, 87, argues that Tlepolemus "assumes seven different identities or characterizations, the last of which reveals that the first three were outright lies and the rest were tricks calculated to destroy the band and rescue the maiden."

aspect of the theme of 'metamorphosis' within the narrative, as both the novel's title and prologue make clear. Moreover, role-shifting points to role-mirroring, which exposes multiformity associated with a world of appearances. The underlying premise of this study is that the narrative of the *Metamorphoses* revolves around a series of transformations of a simple basic unit. In the last book, however, the goddess Isis allows Lucius to leave the world of appearances and enter a world that is essentially uniform, thus providing a stark contrast with what has preceded. Since the goddess of many names admits of only one identity for herself, her anamorphosis of Lucius further helps to characterize his earlier adventures as belonging to a realm of bewildering deceptions.

Furthermore, throughout the narrative several characters construct schemes and/or assume disguises. The enactment of these involves an assumption and performance of roles.[4] Quasi-comic schemes and/or disguises are also seen in the genre of Greek New Comedy and Roman Comedy, and thus help to define the *Metamorphoses* as comic novel.

I am in debt to Greimasian narrative theory for my analysis of the novel from the perspective of 'roles' and 'performances.'[5] Although the theory was originally developed for narratives, it has

---

[4] For an analysis of the tale of Apuleius' Cupid and Psyche as a New Comedy plot see Frangoulidis 1997, 145-77.

[5] The only available and most illuminating presentation of Greimas' theory in English is that by Philippides 1994. (Greimas and Courtés 1982, presents the theory in dictionary form, subdivided into entries.) A brief discussion also appears in Elam 1980, 126-131. Otherwise, the reader is left to reconstruct Greimas' theory from his application in *Maupassant* (Greimas 1988).

Introduction

become a suitable methodological tool for interpreting dramatic texts as well.[6]

According to Greimas, the syntactical arrangement of narrative is based on a structure constituted by a model of interrelating actants, all of which lie below the discursive level. The term 'actant' designates a syntactic position within a structure of reticular units devoid of any content.[7] In this context actants may be understood as empty boxes. Greimas terms the syntactical organization of the narrative as 'actantial model' and 'surface structure.' He also holds that there is a deeper structure, the semiotic square, which is constituted by fundamental semiotic units of the type, 'life' vs 'death' and 'non-death' vs 'non-life.' Greimas identifies up to six actants and orders their arrangement in the actantial structure in the following way:[8]

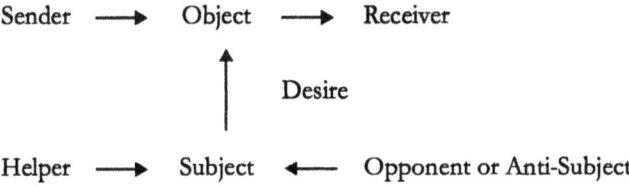

The actant-sender designates the giver of orders; the receiver signifies the character who benefits from these orders; the subject implies the character who is carrying out the deeds. The object designates the goal/value of the subject-actant to possess the object; the helper defines the actant working in the direction of the

---

[6] Philippides 1984; Calame 1995; Ubersfeld 1996, 43-87; see also Elam 1980, 126-131.
[7] Greimas and Courtés 1982, 4 (s.v. *actant*).
[8] Greimas 1984, 207; Philippides 1994, 112.

subject; and, finally, the actant-opponent and/or anti-subject specifies an actant working against the direction of the subject. The desire of the actant-subject to gain possession of the actant-object constitutes the function of the 'narrative program' and, therefore, advances the plot.[9]

On the level of discourse, all these actants become concrete *actors*, executing roles assigned to them by the narrative.[10] The combination of at least one actantial role (i.e. position in the actantial structure) with one thematic role constitutes the actor, who is thus endowed at one and the same time with a *modus operandi* and a *modus essendi*.[11] These actors may be an individual (for example, John), or collective (for instance, a crowd). They may be either figurative (anthropomorphic or zoomorphic), or non-figurative (e.g. fortune).[12]

Within the syntactic organization of the narrative, any given actor can fill the position of more than one actant and thus occupy more than one position in the actantial model.[13] For example, in the *noverca* tale (Book 10), the *noverca* or stepmother falls in love

---

[9] Greimas and Courtés 1982, 245-46 (s.v. *narrative program*); Philippides 1994, 114. For an analysis of the carpet-scene in Aeschylus' *Agamemnon* in terms of two contrasting Greimasian 'narrative programs,' see Philippides 1984; for further applications in Classical texts see Calame 1995.

[10] Greimas 1984, 211-13; Philippides 1994, 112.

[11] Greimas and Courtés 1982, 8 (s.v. *actorialization*). The use of the term 'actor' by Greimas derives from the Latin word *actor*, meaning 'doer' and not the French term actor, meaning actor.

[12] Greimas and Courtés 1982, 7 (s.v. *actor*); Philippides 1994, 114. In literary semiotics the term actor replaces that of an individual character or *'dramatis persona'* because it can apply not only to humans, but also animals or concepts. On this see: Greimas and Courtés 1982, 5 (s.v. *actant*); and Philippides 1994, 111-12.

[13] Philippides 1994, 114.

Introduction

with her stepson. The actor stepmother may also appear in the position of the actant-receiver, since she is the beneficiary of her desires. In the same way, the actor stepson, who fills the position of the object, may also appear in the position of the actant-sender, since he inspires his stepmother's passion for him. On the other hand, many actors fill the position of only one actant. In the tale of Thrasyleon (Book 4), the robbers who present Thrasyleon the bear to Demochares appear only in the position of the helper.

I have replaced the Greimasian term 'narrative program' with less theoretical terms, such as 'plan,' 'plot' and/or 'scheme,' so as not to discourage interested non-theoretical readers. In the case of a 'plan' actors execute their roles as their own true selves, while in a 'plot' and/or 'scheme' actors execute their plans by assuming a persona that is not their own, thus executing two roles: their own and the additional one assumed within the narrative as part of the 'plot'/'scheme.'

In the present study I define 'role' as the distinct features which the narrative endows the actors/characters with at any given point in the novel's discourse.[14] The substance of this role conditions narrative action, as actors are expected to do certain things associated with the role they assume. In other words, the

---

[14] Greimas and Courtés 1982, 343-44 (s.v. *thematic*). My definition of the terms 'auctor,' maker, and 'actor,' differs from those scholars, such as Winkler (1985) and Hijmans Jr. *et al.* (1995), who employ the same terms in their narratological readings of the *Metamorphoses*. The latter focus on the various narrative voices in the text and their skillful interaction. By contrast, I examine the constant shift of roles by almost all major actors/characters in the narrative. A concise explication of this kind of narratology appears in Hijmans Jr. *et al.* 1995, 7-12. For a brilliant narratological reading of *The Golden Ass* and the interplay between *auctor* and *actor* see Winkler 1985.

term 'role' makes the narrative progress, adding meaning to it, whereas the notion of 'position in the actantial structure' explains the organization of the narrative. For instance, when Thelyphron assumes the role of guard, he is expected to do certain things associated with keeping watch. In certain instances several roles are assigned to one actor. Lucius first appears in the role of traveler going to Thessaly on business, but is subsequently transformed into an ass, as a result of his unbounded interest in magic and his pursuit of slavish pleasures. His transformation into an animal through magic constitutes a new role assigned to him by the narrative. This differs considerably from subsequent roles, such as playing the miller's human helper, which Lucius willingly assumes in the course of his asinine adventures (Book 9). The protagonist's restoration to human form suggests the assumption of yet another role, as Lucius is entirely different from his earlier animal form. He then acts out the role of neophyte, as a priest first of Isis and later of her brother/consort Osiris. When the latter elects Lucius to the college of *pastophori*, his promotion within the clerical hierarchy may also be seen as a variation on his role as simple priest. In this role as pastophor, Lucius exercizes both his religious and civic duties, proudly displaying his baldness and therefore making clear his role as an Isiac priest.

To take another example, in the Thelyphron tale (Book 2), the protagonist first appears as a penniless youth, on his way to watch the Olympic games. He then takes on the role of guardian of the corpse against the witches who plunder dead bodies to use in their wicked arts. The earlier reference to his lack of money is designed to explain his eager assumption of the role as guard of the corpse. During the wake, Thelyphron's face is mutilated by witches, implying a change in appearance and thus yet another role. Finally, Thelyphron alters his looks by growing his hair and putting a patch or 'mask' on his nose, and thus conceals his deformed face. It is in this role that we first encounter him in the narrative: Thelyphron is ridiculed by guests at a banquet held by Byrrhene, an aunt of Lucius, when she asks him to relate the story of his mutilation by the witches.

I define 'performance' as the actions undertaken by the actors/characters in order to achieve the object of their goals/values.[15] The term 'performance' is intimately associated with the notion of 'role,' as the former becomes a manifestation of the latter. In the Thelyphron tale, for instance, the actions undertaken by the protagonist to achieve this goal constitute his performance, which may either succeed or fail. To take another example, in Book 7 Tlepolemus the groom disguises himself as Haemus the brigand, and succeeds in liberating his bride Charite from captivity in the robbers' cave, because he acts in accordance with the demands of his role. In the end, however, Tlepolemus himself also falls victim to Thrasyllus' trickery and meets a tragic death. In the Thelyphron tale, the protagonist overestimates his abilities and foolishly undertakes the role of guardian of the corpse. Thelyphron's inability to comprehend the dangers of his role leads to the horrific mutilation of his face by the witches during the vigil. Thus Apuleius offers a variety of performances in the work. In spite of their apparent success at the outset, almost all performances fail in the end, the only true exceptions being those by Lucius as an Isiac devotee in Book 11. In this way the narrative

---

[15] See Greimas and Courtés 1982, 226-28 (s.v. *performance*).

of the *Metamorphoses* makes clear that there is no hope of salvation in the world outside Isis' domain and protection.

In this study I am especially interested in the intersection of plans or schemes with one another; the overlapping of distinct plots determines the shift of the characters' position in the actantial structure and thus adds an ironic meaning to the narrative. At the same time, it aligns with the novel's basic theme of metamorphosis.

In the opening tale, for example, Aristomenes devises a plan to save Socrates from his affair with the witch Meroe. Aristomenes here plays the role of friend, but the execution of his plan involves performance and triggers Meroe's decision to exact revenge on her lover for deserting her. Meroe's actions may also be defined as a plan, in which Aristomenes is to fill the helper's position, leading his friend to death and then burying him when he dies. Aristomenes, however, fails to realize this change of circumstances and his resultant change of role. He thus urges his friend to depart, in the belief that he is helping Socrates to safety. In actual fact he is inadvertently acting as Socrates' opponent, by assisting in the realization of Meroe's plan. In this way, Aristomenes may be said to be turning from Socrates' friend into his unwitting enemy. The tale then emphasizes the ironic and mysterious workings of magic, which humans are so incapable of comprehending that they cannot save themselves without divine help.

Similarly, in the tale of Thrasyleon (Book 4), the protagonist assumes the disguise of a bear as part of the robbers' stratagem to enter the house of the rich Demochares and plunder it. In his role as bear, the robber Thrasyleon takes the place of the subject, whose object is to help his colleagues to infiltrate Demochares'

Introduction

house and rob it. In the meantime Demochares himself is engaged in elaborate preparations for the production of a splendid *munus gladiatorium* to please the crowd of Plataeans. In parallel with the robbers' plot, Demochares' preparations may also be defined as a plan. It suffers a serious setback when all the bears die from inactivity, heat and the outbreak of an epidemic. Nevertheless, contrary to the prevailing view that the elaborate arrangements for the *munus gladiatorium* achieve no results within the narrative, Thrasyleon's performance as a bear ironically provides the missing element in the production of Demochares' spectacle and thus sets it in motion within the tale's action. In the performance of this spectacle, Thrasyleon/bear ceases to be the subject in the robbers' scheme to rob the rich man's house and turns into the object of pursuit in Demochares' spectacle. In this pursuit, Thrasyleon/bear is killed and the robbers' elaborate disguise is exposed.

At this point it should be stressed that I depart from Greimas in that I am not interested in the deeper structure of the narrative—the semiotic square—for that goes beyond the scope of the present study. I examine instances in which both Lucius and other secondary characters in the novel act out roles assigned to them by the narrative. Moreover, I do not present the character administration in the actantial structure of every plan or scheme of the narrative, for that would give a technical character to my work. Plans may either be complex, i.e. presupposing the preliminary realization of other plans, or simple. Moreover, these plans may multiply, depending on the actions each character undertakes in a given narrative sequence. As said above, I am especially interested in instances where two plans or schemes develop simultaneously and/or overlap with one another. Such intersections determine the shift in the original position of characters in the actantial structure; the resultant redistribution of roles leads to situations actors/characters cannot comprehend and thus guard themselves against appropriately. Finally, the present study does not claim to be exhaustive –it merely intends to elucidate the concepts of 'roles' and 'performances' by examining a representative selection of embedded tales and longer narrative sequences from the novel.

Structurally speaking, the entire narrative of the novel may be regarded as a triptych consisting of: a) the pre-metamorphosis sequence, where the emphasis falls on magic (humans vs witches) and the punishment of curiosity (Books 1-3.24); b) the lengthy post-metamorphosis sequence in which the emphasis is primarily on human affairs (humans vs humans or animals) and the punishment of excess (Books 3.25-10); and c) the reformation sequence where the emphasis is on religion (man and god) and divine reward (Book 11). In the first sequence, the catastrophic power of magic is responsible for all the transformations the characters undergo within the narrative. In the second, the emphasis primarily falls on disguise and deception but less frequently on magic, as humans are unable to bring about transformations in the way witches can. In the first two sequences then it seems that two main vices are highlighted throughout: lust (Socrates / Lucius / *matrona* / Thrasyllus, etc.) and avarice (Thelyphron / the robbers / the widow / Thrasyleon, etc.). In the third sequence, however, the emphasis centers on the positive and beneficent magic represented by Isis.

As far as actantial structures are concerned, in the first two sequences the various characters of the narrative have distinct plans with distinct goals/objects. The intersection of these plans creates tension in the narrative. In the third sequence, however, man and god develop plans along similar lines, thus revealing Isis' uniform world.

Chapter One, *Unwittingly Successful Performances: The Triumph of Magic*, discusses three narrative sequences: the Tales of Aristomenes (1.5-19), the Tale of Thelyphron (2.21-30), and the longer narrative unit of the Laughter festival and Lucius' metamorphosis into an ass (3.1-27). In all three cases, several main characters seem to be victims both of passion and witchcraft. Moreover, these characters inadvertently engage in performances as a result of the intervention of magic. Their unwitting role-playing has a lasting impact on most of them. The sequences thus have a cautionary function, intended to warn Lucius, the primary narrator, about the dangers of both magic and lust. Yet these warnings go unheeded. In fact, Lucius has already made a decision to become deliberately involved in an affair with the witch Fotis, a lowly slave of the witch Pamphile, so as to gain access to magic. Ironically, although the protagonist originally wanted to become a bird and fly around his mistress Fotis, his involvement in witchcraft results in his being transformed into an ass. This metamorphosis constitutes a new role, not chosen by Lucius himself, but rather one imposed on him by the narrative.

Chapter Two, *Fatally Successful Performances*, examines roles assumed by Tlepolemus, Thrasyllus and Charite in the lengthy narrative sequence known as the Charite-complex (4.22-8.14): Tlepolemus disguises himself as Haemus the brigand in order to liberate his bride, who was abducted by the robbers on her wedding night. Having punished the abductors for their greed, he is finally wedded to his bride. Like Tlepolemus, Charite later exacts revenge on the libidinous suitor Thrasyllus for 'abducting' her husband, with whom she is subsequently (re)united, albeit in death. Her suicide is predictable, since it is the only way to bring about this 'reunion.' Moreover, Charite's scheme to exact vengeance on Thrasyllus for murdering her husband and harboring sexual ambitions towards her is enhanced by wedding imagery, as are the ensuing suicides of both bride and suitor. All of these 'marriages' end in disaster, an outcome which underlines the fact that there is no marital bliss in the world of Lucius' adventures.

Chapter Three, *Unsuccessful Performances*, attempts to illuminate the concept of unsuccessful role-playing by concentrating on two narrative sequences: first, the adultery tale of the miller's wife (9.14-31); and second, the *noverca* tale (10.2-12). Both wives pretend to be faithful, but in reality they both commit adultery, thus revealing their lust. The disclosure soon afterwards of their immoral activities exposes their wicked mores and, by implication, the falsehood and hypocrisy in the world of Lucius' adventures as an ass.

Chapter Four, *Man and Animal*, discusses instances where humans act as animals and vice versa. In the Thrasyleon tale (4.14-21), the protagonist assumes the role of a bear in order to help the robbers infiltrate the house of the rich Demochares and rob it. Through his performance as a bear, Thrasyleon ironically provides the missing element in Demochares' spectacle and thus meets a fatal death, while his disguise is exposed. In contrast, towards the end of his adventures (10.16-35), the ass assumes the role of a human being. This behavior may be interpreted as rehearsal in anticipation of his imminent restoration to human form in the subsequent Book. His successful performance as a human ironically prompts his new master Thiasos to exhibit him in the Corinthian theater, as show piece in a sex show with a mass murderess sentenced to be thrown *ad bestias*. Moreover, the narrative of the spectacle may appear to mimetically re-enact distinct stages of transition and marital rites: the choral dance of pretty boys and girls may be interpreted as marking the transition from puberty to adulthood; the pantomime of Paris' Judgment may be read as a betrothal scene as Venus promises to give Paris a wife like herself in beauty, i.e. Helen; and the 'marriage' of the ass with the mass murderess may represent consummation. The ass' fear of the wild beasts in the arena leads to his refusal to have sex with the convict and explains the ensuing secret exit from the theater. This exit unawares puts an end to the long chain of asinine adventures which began with his 'marriage' to the slave Fotis. Moreover, as Paris' Judgment represents the most celebrated case of divine intervention in human affairs, it may be taken as foreshadowing Isis' intervention in the next book. Lucius' ensuing initiation into her priesthood after his reformation may be interpreted as a form of divine marriage.[16] The connection is reinforced as Isis shares some features with Venus. All this lies in stark contrast to Paris, who brings destruction on both himself and his entire race through his ensuing marriage to Helen, a spit image of Venus.

The concluding chapter, *Successful Performances: Lucius' Spiritual Journey*, interprets the Spring festival of the launching of Isis' new ship as a metaphor for Lucius' entrance into his new life, culminating in his anamorphosis and initiation into Isis'

---

[16] Lateiner 2000, 326.

priesthood. The theme of constant 'rebirth' is underlined by the repetition of themes from the ship-launching narrative in all three initiations into the priesthood. Such a theme is alien to the world of the asinine adventures, where the emphasis lies on the continuous presence of death. Moreover, Lucius' integration into the Isiac fellowship contrasts with his earlier refusal to integrate into the Hypatan community and their 'fellowship of Laughter' following his performance in the Laughter festival. The reason offered is that the Hypatans' god of Laughter presents Lucius with sorrows and reduces him to tears, unlike Isis, who grants her initiate joy and the prospect of bliss. Lucius' initiation into Isis' priesthood involves celibacy and thus is set in direct opposition to his earlier 'marriage' to the slave Fotis, which brought about his metamorphosis into an ass and his ensuing misadventures. Thus, the narrative of the *Metamorphoses* makes it clear that there is no salvation outside the harmonious domain of Isis' protection, in which the goals of man and god coincide.

CHAPTER I

Unwittingly Successful Performances: The Triumph of Magic

In this chapter I discuss instances of unintentional performances in three narrative sequences: (1) The Tale of Aristomenes (1.5-19), (2) The Tale of Thelyphron (2.21-30), and (3) the narrative of the Laughter festival (3.1-12) and Lucius' ensuing transformation into an ass (3.13-27). All these three sequences are carefully positioned in the narrative. In the first tale, the sub-narrator Aristomenes tells of how his friend Socrates falls victim to magic. In the second tale, the sub-narrator Thelyphron relates the story of his own mutilation by witches. Thirdly, the Laughter festival narrative involves the primary narrator Lucius falling prey to magic. Moreover, most of the main characters in these sequences are victims both of passion and magic. Lucius fails to comprehend the dangers that lurk in magic, let alone learn anything from his horrible experience in the Laughter festival, which is in itself a consequence of his own accidental contact with sorcery. Instead, he has already made a conscious decision to involve himself in an affair with a slave, the witch Fotis; following the Laughter festival he pursues magic with the same misguided zeal as before and is changed into an ass as a result. His metamorphosis into an animal marks the beginning of his woeful adventures within the novel; these only end with Isis' intervention in the final book, when she delivers him from magic and restores him to human form.

1. From Friend to Unwitting Enemy: Aristomenes' Tale of Socrates

On his way to Hypata, Lucius sees two travelers walking ahead of him: the narrator of the tale, later named Aristomenes, and his nameless companion. The latter expresses skepticism in the tale, as if to suggest that there is more to the account than first meets the eye.[17] The tale relates the death of Aristomenes' friend Socrates, following his affair with Meroe the witch. Lucius joins the company of the two travelers and seeks to discover their topic of conversation. The well-educated Lucius, in his curiosity to learn Aristomenes' tale of magic, indirectly advances the novel's plot. He urges his fellow traveler to retell the tale and even offers to treat him to a meal upon their arrival at the first inn. The offer is accepted and Aristomenes begins his account of events (1.2-20). His retelling has a therapeutic effect, as it helps him purge his anxiety and sense of guilt over his unwitting complicity in the murder of his friend, whom he had intended to save.

In the tale the sub-narrator Aristomenes (hereafter narrator) devises a plan to save his friend Socrates from Meroe the witch. Ironically this sets into motion Meroe's own plan to exact vengeance on her unfaithful lover for deserting her. Rather than kill Aristomenes, Meroe plots to make him an accomplice in Socrates' death, by assigning him the (hostile) role of burying him when he dies. Unbeknown to him, Aristomenes is thus rendered a foe rather than a friend. This transformation mirrors Meroe's earlier change from Socrates' mistress to his antagonist, when she reduces her lover to her slave and then exacts terrible revenge on

---

[17] Ruebel 2000, xv (foreword by Steve Nimis).

him. Moreover, in his capacity as Meroe's helper, Aristomenes also assumes the role of Panthia, who aids her sister Meroe in carrying out the 'sacrifice' of Socrates in the earlier part of the tale. This set of similarities makes Aristomenes in some sense a double of the witches, albeit with one major difference: whereas the sisters act consciously, Aristomenes unintentionally collaborates in the murder of his friend. In turn, Aristomenes' complicity explains his present anxiety and sense of guilt.

Scholarly discussions of the tale have mainly concentrated on the way this episode of the *Metamorphoses* does not make sense, interpreting it either as an indication of Apuleius' careless workmanship,[18] or as a mark of the breakdown in the pattern of causality.[19] Others have sought to establish a connection between the fate suffered by Socrates because of involvement in magic and Lucius' experience in the larger narrative;[20] several others have noted the neoteric and elegiac echoes in Aristomenes' pathetic invocation to his bed.[21] In what follows, I shall focus on the clever shift of roles by all the major characters in the tale resulting from the execution of Meroe's vengeful plan.[22]

---

[18] Perry 1967, 259-264.
[19] Shumate 1996 (a), 71-74.
[20] Schlam 1992, 67-68; Tatum 1969, 493-502; Scobie 1978, 50-51; Murgatroyd 2001, 41.
[21] Mattiacci 1998, 129 and 148; Mattiacci 1993, 257-267, and Westerbrink 1978, 64.
[22] Only Schlam 1992, 41 observed that "his (i.e. Aristomenes') attempt to help him (i.e. Socrates) results in his death," but did not develop the idea further. An interesting reading of the tale from the perspective of the constant reinterpretation of its incredible events has been advanced by Winkler 1985, 82-86. For illumination of the concepts of Greek and Roman friendship, see Konstan 1996, 71-94, and Konstan 1995, 328-342, respectively. On the

At the outset of the tale, Aristomenes is traveling to Hypata to buy cheese of excellent quality at a modest price. His role as traveler evokes Lucius, who is also on the way to Thessaly on a business trip. When Aristomenes arrives at Hypata, he discovers that a fellow merchant named Lupus has already emptied the market. Such wolfish behavior is entirely consistent with the merchant's name, and can perhaps be considered the first instance of human to animal 'metamorphosis' in the novel.[23] Aristomenes reveals his belief in superstition when he states that he had set out on his trip 'on the wrong foot' (1.5): *sinistro pede profectum me*. In its turn, this image anticipates the still greater misfortune awaiting him in town as a result of his involvement in magic. Aristomenes' tale of the supernatural thus serves as a warning to Lucius against the reckless interest he has already displayed in the subject.

To his amazement, Aristomenes runs into an old friend in the marketplace. Socrates is alive but in a terrible state, as he is seated on the ground soliciting coins from passers-by for his mistress. In 1.6 Aristomenes describes Socrates' paleness using the term *deformatus*, which is taken from the language of metamorphosis.[24] Later, in 1.6, he explicitly presents his complexion as *larvale simulacrum*. Aristomenes explains to Socrates that his family has given him up for dead and has already mourned him. This situation anticipates a similar one in Book 11, in which Lucius is believed by his family to have died. Although Socrates is

---

association between the themes of mutilation and lameness, see Paschalis 1992, 125-126.

[23] Kenney 1998, 220; Keulen 2000, 320.

[24] *OLD*, s.v. *deformo*, 4; van der Paardt 1978, 82, considers Socrates' change as the first instance of metamorphosis in the tale.

Unwittingly Successful Performances: The Triumph of Magic

at first unwilling to leave his begging bowl in the market, Aristomenes raises him from the ground and offers him a cloak. The two men go first to the baths and then to an inn, where Aristomenes treats his companion with abundant food and wine. All these actions help to characterize Aristomenes as a true friend. Having overcome his initial reticence, Socrates tells of the misfortune he has suffered at the hands of his mistress. In donning Aristomenes' cloak—or 'costume'—and confiding in him, Socrates moves out of the role of Meroe's pawn and into a new one as friend.

In his own tale Socrates first appears as spectator on his way to watch a gladiatorial fight. Returning home one day from a business trip to Macedonia, he falls victim to robbers near Larissa who attack him and take all his money.[25] The purpose of his travels makes Socrates a fitting target for the thieves, who leave him in such a wretched condition that he seeks refuge in a nearby inn kept by Meroe. In the beginning his new-found landlady takes good care of him (1.7): *nimis quam humane*, as if to reflect Aristomenes' kind behavior after the surprise encounter in the marketplace (1.6). Socrates' woes begin after Meroe lures him into her bed in the inn, an episode which foreshadows the misery to befall him after spending the night with Aristomenes, yet again in an inn. Within the context of this interpretation, Meroe assumes the position previously held by the robbers. In 1.7, Socrates actually identifies Meroe as worse than the robbers, since she took his clothes, which the bandits did not, as well as all the money he

---

[25] In book 2, Thelyphron falls victim to the evils of magic in Thessaly, on his way to watch the Olympic games (21): *ad spectaculum Olympicum*.

earned as a sack-carrier: *et ipsas etiam lacinias, quas boni latrones contegendo mihi concesserant, in eam contuli, operulas etiam, quas adhuc vegetus saccariam faciens merebam.*

This implicit association of Meroe with the band of robbers explains her subsequent violent behavior in the company of Panthia. The two witches burst in on the companions to butcher Socrates in his sleep. Having initially intended to be a spectator at a gladiatorial fight, Socrates thus ironically becomes a spectacle himself after sleeping with the witch. If anything, Socrates is punished not for seeking refuge after being attacked, but for agreeing so readily to sleep with Meroe. Thus he is a victim both of passion and witchcraft, just like Lucius after him.

Aristomenes criticizes his friend for getting involved in an affair with an old whore, but Socrates informs him that Meroe is a witch with powers superior to those of the gods (1.8):

> '[s]aga,' inquit, 'et divini potens caelum deponere, terram suspendere, fontes durare, montes diluere, manes sublimare, deos infirmare, sidera extinguere, Tartarum ipsum inluminare.'

> 'A witch,' he replied, 'with supernatural power: she can lower the sky and suspend the earth, solidify fountains and dissolve mountains, raise up ghosts and bring down gods, darken the stars and light up Tartarus itself.'

Here the witches are said to possess supernatural powers capable of controlling the entire universe. There is no mention, however, that these powerful beings can make their lovers yield to their lust. Aristomenes expresses disbelief in Meroe's supernatural powers, just as the unnamed companion earlier voiced his own skepticism in Aristomenes' tale. Ignoring a friendly exhortation to abandon his tragic mode of narration, Socrates goes on to recount several exploits testifying to Meroe's vindictiveness on uncooperative lovers and enemies alike, whenever her status as a woman or authority is questioned (1.9-10).[26] The similarities between Socrates' story and the narrator's tale make the former an example of a *mise en abyme* of, or paradigm for, the latter.[27]

On the level of the tale's delivery, Socrates' telling Aristomenes the story of his misfortune with Meroe resembles Aristomenes' relating the tale of Socrates' death and his own involvement in it to his own internal audience and by extension the novel's readers. Furthermore, in relating his tale of woes after accepting hospitality from Aristomenes, Socrates resembles his host, who recounts his story for his fellow travelers and by extension for us, the novel's readers, following the offer of a meal paid for by Lucius. When the narrator agrees with Lucius' proposal and tells his tale, he, in effect, turns into a literary merchant, telling his story to his audience of fellow travelers and to us, the readers of the novel.

Upon hearing the tale, Aristomenes is filled with terror lest Meroe should learn of their private exchange. Nevertheless, he fails to comprehend Meroe's supernatural powers and devises a plan to save his friend, which involves retiring to bed early and then leaving at dawn, *antelucio* (1.11).[28] Aristomenes truly believes he will be able to save his friend. His plan, like Meroe's subsequent revenge on Socrates, involves performance.

---

[26] A good assessment of the function of Socrates' inserted tale from a narratological perspective now appears in Murgatroyd 2001, 40-46.

[27] For a definition of the term *mise en abyme* see Prince 1987, 53.

[28] *Pace* Tatum 1969, 495, who thinks that Aristomenes is aware of the invincible powers Meroe possesses.

In the actantial model, the actor/character administration may appear as follows: Aristomenes fills the subject position as *auctor*, maker of the plan to save his friend, precisely as Meroe identifies him later in 1.12: *fugae huius auctor*. Aristomenes' goal/object is to lead his friend to safety; Socrates fills the place of the receiver, since he benefits from the plan. Aristomenes also occupies the helper position, while the witch that of the opponent.

In the enactment of the plan, Socrates goes to bed and immediately falls into a deep sleep induced by his earlier drinking, while Aristomenes locks the doors of the room and puts his bed against them as protection against the witch.[29] Although Socrates has been enslaved to Meroe and is already emaciated, the escape plan appears to alter his lot, given that it precipitates his death. Thus Aristomenes fails to learn any lesson from the earlier account of Meroe's exploits (1.9-10).

At around the third night watch, the doors of the room burst open, causing Aristomenes' bed to overturn on his head. As he falls on the ground, he comically observes that he has been transformed into a tortoise (1.12): *de Aristomene testudo factus*.[30] The choice of this particular animal for the 'metamorphosis' is significant, as tortoises are notoriously slow and suggest the formal annulment of Aristomenes' plan, which depends on traveling fast. From the vantage point under his bed, Aristomenes sees two old women entering the room, one holding a lantern, the other a

---

[29] Dowden 1998, 12, develops an association between safety from magic and being awake: "[t]here is no hope for Socrates, who *iam sopitus stertebat altius* ('by now was fast asleep and snoring deeply' 1,11). Aristomenes on the other hand through fear stays awake (*invigilo*) at first for some while."

[30] On this see recent comments in Murgatroyd 2001, 45-46.

sword, and overhears their exchange. This highlights the eyewitness quality of the events he recounts in his tale (1.12). Structurally speaking, the exchange of the sisters in the room (1.12) balances the earlier exchange between Socrates and Aristomenes (1.7-10).

In her dialogue with Panthia, Meroe boasts of her superior treatment of Socrates, comparing her love for him with that of the Moon and Jupiter in their respective affairs with the young mortals Endymion and Ganymedes (1.12). The comparison is clearly intended as a 'correction' of Socrates' negative portrayal of her in his own exchange with Aristomenes.[31] Meroe goes on to reveal awareness of her former lover's role in slandering her and conspiring to flee; this feature contrasts with Socrates' behavior in 1.8, when he expresses concern for secrecy. However, she errs in thinking that her lover wants to abandon her on account of her advanced age.[32] In 1.7 Socrates praised her attractiveness in old age: *anum, sed admodum scitulam*, as if offering an explanation for his subsequent involvement in a long-term affair with her (*annosam* 1.7). Finally, Meroe expresses her disapproval of Calypso, who spent the rest of her life wailing after Ulysses abandoned her by use of cunning. She thus prefigures her role as a vindictive witch— a role familiar to the tale's internal and external audience from Socrates' earlier narrative of her exploits (1.9-10).[33] Meroe then

---

[31] Harrison 1990, 194-195, brings out Meroe's claim to divinity in accordance with Socrates' earlier characterization of her as *femina divina* (1.8).

[32] Meroe's concern for her age points to the goddess Venus, who expresses a similar concern in the tale of Cupid and Psyche. On this see Frangoulidis 1997, 162.

[33] In relation to the epic model of the episode, Harrison 1990, 194-195, nicely points out that Meroe here signals her intention not to behave like

turns to Aristomenes, whom she identifies as the *auctor*, maker of the plan to take Socrates away, thus revealing her knowledge of what was supposed to be secret. Panthia proposes to tear Aristomenes apart or castrate him, making clear that she views him as an opponent too. Yet Meroe resolves to spare his life, so that he may assist in the burial of his friend. This foreshadows Aristomenes' subsequent role as helper in the continuation of her revenge, which occurs in the second part of the tale (1.13): *qui miselli huius corpus parvo contumelet humo.*

The violent intrusion of the witches into the room marks a radical shift in the narrative from the plan devised by Aristomenes to that executed by Meroe. In the second situation all actors or characters assume new positions in the actantial structure: Meroe occupies the double position of the subject and receiver, her object being to exact revenge on Socrates. Aristomenes could perhaps be regarded as filling the position of the opponent, yet his repeated use of verbs of seeing, *video* (1.12), *aspexi* (1.13), underlines his passive role, as he does nothing to prevent the witches from performing their sacrifice of the sleeping Socrates. This passivity is also reminiscent of the role Socrates originally intended to assume as spectator of the gladiatorial games. Meroe foreshadows Aristomenes' subsequent replacement of Panthia in the role of helper, as she assigns him the role of burying Socrates when he dies.

In the ensuing narrative of Meroe's punishment of Socrates, McCreight has pointed out the presence of features alluding to

---

Calypso, but to show the resolution of Circe. For literary parallels between Socrates and Odysseus, see Münstermann 1995, 8-13.

animal-sacrifice rites.³⁴ Firstly, Socrates' agreement to spend the night in the inn with Aristomenes before leaving the next morning corresponds to the ritual detail of animals going to the sacrificial site on their own initiative.³⁵ Secondly, in turning Socrates' head to the left Meroe fulfills the ritualistic requirement of the animal's implicit consent to the slaughter.³⁶ Thirdly, the collection of blood in a bottle following the insertion of a sword in the victim's neck evokes the sacrificial procedure of cutting the animal's throat and collecting its blood in a basin (1.13).³⁷ Finally, the narrator concurs with such a view when he relates that Meroe pulls out Socrates' heart and examines it in a manner reminiscent of the ritualistic observation of animal *exta* (1.13): *ne quid demutaret, credo, a victimae religione.*³⁸ McCreight interprets these features as designed to add a horrifying yet comic tone to the narrative, since a man rather than an animal is sacrificed.³⁹ However, in a tale so concerned with animal metamorphosis, the superimposition of imagery borrowed from the animal-sacrifice rite may also suggest Socrates' implicit transformation into a beast.⁴⁰ As such, it forms a thematic link with Aristomenes' earlier transformation into a tortoise, as well as with Meroe's other lover's metamorphosis into a beaver, related by

---

³⁴ McCreight 1993, 53-56.
³⁵ For the procedure see Burkert 1985, 56-57.
³⁶ Burkert 1985, 56.
³⁷ For the practice see Burkert 1985, 56; for an artistic representation of this practice in Roman imperial reliefs, see the references in McCreight 1993, 55.
³⁸ McCreight 1993, 56.
³⁹ McCreight 1993, 53.
⁴⁰ For the reversal of the sacrificial motif, in which the animal is endowed with human characteristics, thus resulting in ambiguities in the narrative, see Philippides 1984, 72-106, Ch. III.

Socrates earlier in his tale of her exploits (1.9-10).[41] On a broader level, Socrates' slaughter may be read as the symbolic 'butchering' of Aristomenes' plan to save his friend.

Socrates does not die when Meroe pulls out his heart and examines it, but is destined to survive until the next day on the road. Such a delay is made possible by Panthia's insertion of a sponge in the wound, with the explicit instruction to return to the sea through a river (1.13): *'heus tu,' inquit, 'spongia, cave in mari nata per fluvium transeas.'* Like her sister before her, Panthia assigns a role to the sponge, which not only helps to conceal Socrates' wound, but also prolongs his life until the conditions of his death are fully met. The following day, Aristomenes directs his friend to a river to quench his thirst, upon which the sponge falls out in accordance with Panthia's instructions. Although Meroe is the true murderer, in this way she deliberately postpones Socrates' death so as to make Aristomenes deliver the final blow. Having committed their crime, the sisters empty their bladders over Aristomenes' face, emphasizing their control over him, and then depart never to reappear.[42] Upon their departure the door slams shut, thus marking the end of their act in the earlier part of the tale.

The narrative of the witches' entry into the room spells out both the conditions under which Socrates will die and his companion's role in it. Yet through his mistaken belief that

---

[41] In the context of Aristomenes' business trip to Hypata, as murderess of Socrates Meroe may be seen as taking the position of Aristomenes' competitor, Lupus, who empties the market. Carrying this association a step further, the failure of Aristomenes' plan to save his friend re-enacts the failure of his cheese-buying trip.

[42] Scobie 1975, 109 (*s.v. uesicam exonerant*), observes that: "urinating around or on someone prevented a person from escaping from a particular situation."

Socrates is *already* dead, Aristomenes reveals himself to be an incompetent spectator of the witches' act of murder. He further fears that he will be accused of murder, because nobody will believe his incredible tale (1.14): *cui videbor veri similia dicere proferens vera?*[43] He then reflects on scenarios that would have saved both his friend and himself when the sisters were in the room. These scenarios could only have been acted out if he had assumed the role of Meroe's opponent in her plan, whereas she proves to be the opponent in *his* plan. In this situation, Aristomenes resolves to leave the room at night in order to avoid the punishment that awaits him by law.

Aristomenes' failure to persuade the doorman to open the door so that he may leave and commit suicide has often been interpreted as the awkward insertion of a farcical lover's suicide into a tale of sorcery.[44] Yet, as we will see, Aristomenes' inability to leave and his failure to commit suicide may be said to underline his incapacity to escape from Meroe's revenge plan.

Aristomenes wants to leave the room before daybreak, but he cannot open the door, as the key will not turn in the lock. This situation lies in stark contrast with the witches' earlier violent opening of the same door, thus highlighting his limited abilities when compared to the supernatural powers of the witches. Aristomenes calls out to the doorman sleeping outside and urges him to open up. Ironically enough, the doorman interprets

---

[43] For a valuable discussion of how Apuleius' fictional *Metamorphoses* lays claims to truth, albeit without a discussion of Aristomenes' tale, see Laird 1990, 129-164.

[44] See Perry 1967, 259-264; also Walsh 1970, 150; Scobie 1975, 110 and Smith 1993, 86-87.

Aristomenes' lack of fear of robbers in the streets at night as an indication of involvement in some crime, and does not let him leave for fear of being accused of complicity in murder. Again this situation contrasts with Aristomenes' failure to prevent the witches from leaving the room; in their absence he appears as the perpetrator of the crime and therefore the prime suspect. The doorkeeper goes on to accuse Aristomenes of murdering his roommate and then simply goes back to sleep.

Having abandoned all hope of escape, Aristomenes appeals to his bed to render him some means to commit suicide (1.16):[45]

> 'iam iam grabattule,' inquam, 'animo meo carissime, qui mecum tot aerumnas exanclasti conscius et arbiter, quae nocte gesta sunt, quem solum in meo reatu testem innocentiae citare possum, tu mihi ad inferos festinanti subministra telum salutare.'

> 'The time is now, my little cot,' I said, 'my heart's dearest cot, you who have endured so many tribulations with me, you who know and can judge what happened last night, you who are the only witness I can summon in my trial to testify to my innocence. I am in haste to die: supply me with the weapon that will save me.'

Aristomenes' invocation to his bed calls to mind Panthia's earlier address to the sponge (1.13):

> 'heus tu,' inquit, 'spongia, cave in mari nata per fluvium transeas.'

---

[45] For elements of parody of prayer language in the evocation to the bed, see Westerbrink 1978, 64. Recently, Mattiacci 1998, 129, treats the episode as a parody of the elegiac motif of the *paraclausithyron*. For discussion of the literary *topoi* in this appeal, see Mattiacci 1993, 257-267. On the farcical elements of this episode, see Bajoni 1990, 152.

'[l]isten, o sponge, born in the sea, take care to travel back through a river.'

The connection is reinforced by the fact that Aristomenes' appeal to his bed relates to his death, just as Panthia's instruction to the sponge relates to Socrates' death. The similarity is here intended to highlight a stark contrast between the two different appeals: Panthia succeeds in assigning a role to the sponge, which the latter brilliantly acts out in due course. On the other hand, Aristomenes fails to commit suicide, as the rope he takes from his bed is rotten, and he comically falls on Socrates, rolling him to the ground. The bed that had earlier covered Aristomenes when the witches were in the room does not help him in his present difficulty. Thus Aristomenes' failure on all scores suggests his inability to break out of the role assigned to him by Meroe.

This role is further developed the following morning. At dawn the doorman bursts in, laughing and shouting at Aristomenes to wake up. The abrupt re-opening of the door evokes the earlier violent entry of the witches and thus signals the continuation of their plan in the later part of the tale. Yet Aristomenes proposes a counter-reading of events and surmises that nothing in fact transpired the previous night, because he suddenly sees Socrates rousing from his slumbers. He even fails to notice the fact that he is soaked in urine until Socrates jokingly draws this to his attention.[46] By urinating on Aristomenes, the witches have in a sense turned him into a sponge (making him

---

[46] Panayotakis 1998, 126, advances a rationalistic interpretation of the double dream of Aristomenes and Socrates, "in which bodily oppression and suffocation (symptoms of nightmares) appear in the narrative as aspects of the horrible attack of the witches."

soak up liquid). In this way, he may be seen as no more able to disobey the witches' orders than the sponge is. Nevertheless, Aristomenes continues to believe that the time is ripe for him to carry out the plan to save his friend, and exhorts him to depart (1.17): *'quin imus,' inquam, 'et itineris matutini gratiam capimus?'* This exhortation may be interpreted in precisely the opposite way, as revealing Aristomenes' eagerness to execute his role in leading his friend to death and then burying him when he dies, thus fulfilling Meroe's plan. It is because Aristomenes fails to realize the switch from one plan to the other and the resultant change of role that he unwittingly leads his friend to death.

The execution of the final stage takes place in broad daylight on the open road, in contrast to the foul deed perpetrated by the witches at night in the inn. Having failed to see any wound at the point in Socrates' neck where Meroe plunged her sword, Aristomenes reinterprets the previous night's events as a nightmare caused by excessive eating and drinking. On the other hand, readers of the novel will of course recall that Panthia has concealed the neck wound with the sponge. Aristomenes explains the events by appealing to the authority of those doctors who propose a connection between food and bad dreams. His appeal to medicine is understandable, given that the ancients thought of magic as interconnected with medicine. Socrates also defines his tragic experience the previous night and his present weakness as a bad dream. This is understandable if we consider that Socrates was presented as sleeping when the witches entered the room and performed their 'sacrifice' on him. The misreading of events by both characters involved in the episode allows Aristomenes to maintain the illusion of carrying through his own plan to rescue his friend, whereas he is in fact destined to do quite the opposite.

Scholars have often interpreted the setting of the plane-tree, where Aristomenes directs his friend to sit and have breakfast, as a reference to the Platonic dialogue *Phaedrus*.[47] Socrates' name points to his namesake in Plato's dialogue, as does the setting, which alludes to the *locus amoenus* where Socrates and Phaedrus sit just outside the gates of Athens. The reference to the plane-tree may also be read as a plot element designed to foreshadow the presence of a river nearby, since plane-trees need abundant water. The details of the locale bring to mind the setting where Socrates is expected to meet his death.

Intratextuality reveals a certain similarity between Meroe and Aristomenes, for they both alter the fate of Socrates, yet with one major difference: Aristomenes does so unwittingly. Socrates' pallor towards the end of the tale, after he is offered bread and cheese (1.19: *macie atque pallore buxeo deficientem video*),[48] evokes his ghost-like appearance at the beginning (1.6: *paene alius lurore, ad miseram maciem deformatus*). His present misfortune has come about following the night spent at the inn with his friend, just as his earlier misery with Meroe had begun after his visit to her inn. From this perspective Aristomenes can in some sense be seen as Meroe's double, completing the plan which she did not finish.

---

[47] Drake 2000, 6; Harrison 1998, 57; Schlam 1992, 60; Hanson 1989, 40 and van der Paard 1978, 83. On the other hand, Borghini 1991, 7-14, explores literary associations with death, suggested by the reference to the plane-tree.

[48] For the difficulties of eating both in 1.18-19 and the novel in general, see Heath 1982, 58-59. For intratextuality and the genesis of the term see Sharrock and Morales 2000.

The fear of being accused resurfaces when Aristomenes realizes that there are no travelers on the road to bear witness to his innocence (1.19): *'quis enim de duobus comitum alterum sine alterius noxa peremptum crederet?'*[49] His repeated reference to these fears are designed to persuade his audience, both internal and external, that he did not murder his friend; the earlier skepticism of the unnamed listener warrants such a view. Those of the audience who disagree with Aristomenes' interpretation may view him as unwittingly responsible for Socrates' death. In their eyes, he can be no more than a mere fool, for instead of leading his friend to safety he is working for Meroe in exactly the opposite direction. The tale thus highlights the strange workings of magic, which humans are so totally unable to comprehend that they are powerless to fight against it.

The final tragic development takes place when Aristomenes directs his friend to the spring, so as to quench his thirst after devouring some quantity of bread and cheese (1.19): *'en,' inquam, 'explere latice fontis lacteo.'* It is no accident that this spring is near the plane-tree (1.19): *et haud ita longe radices platani lenis fluvius in speciem placidae paludis ignavus ibat argento vel vitro aemulus in colorem.* The water is described as immovable, clear and silver in color, as if tempting Socrates to drink from it. In contrast to Aristomenes, who is aware of Panthia's words to the sponge, Socrates is ignorant of them, given that he was presented as sleeping when Meroe removed his heart. The moment Socrates bends down to quench his thirst, the

---

[49] Aristomenes' reaction evokes Lucius' choking to death when he put a large pie in his mouth in a cheese-pie competition. For an excellent discussion of this episode, see Winkler 1985, 30-32.

sponge acts out Panthia's earlier instructions, falling from the wound as the victim's lips meet the water. The sponge then appears in the same position as Aristomenes, as they both help to fulfill Meroe's deadly plan. As outlined above, the connection is reinforced by the witches' act of urination. Furthermore, there is also a remarkable contrast between the sponge, which acquires anthropomorphic characteristics and acts as a helper in Meroe's plan, and Socrates, who drops dead as soon as he bends to drink water from the river. This is the point at which Socrates dies, long after his family have mourned him as lost; it contrasts with the episode in Book 11 when Lucius' relatives discover that he is not in fact dead. His death in broad daylight is in agreement with the death of other (honest) characters, such as Tlepolemus, Charite, etc., whose death occurs in the middle of the day. Thus Aristomenes helps to accomplish Panthia's earlier instruction to the sponge, substituting her in the later portion of the tale and leading his friend to death. The presence of the motif of water (river) brings the two characters closer together.

Aristomenes mourns and buries his dead friend. Under normal circumstances this would be considered one of the most pious acts of friendship, yet we know that Meroe spared Aristomenes' life precisely so that he could perform this task (1.13). It can therefore be argued that he is merely acting out his role as the witches' helper or Socrates' opponent in the continuation of her revenge. Thus Meroe's plan is brought to completion, ironically confirming the doorman's earlier accusation that Aristomenes was his companion's murderer.

In his terror Aristomenes does not return to his hometown of Aegion, but relocates to Aetolia, a situation he compares to self-exile (1.19). His self-imposed banishment is motivated by a sense of fear for his own safety and guilt for involvement in the murder of his friend: *quasi conscius mihi caedis humanae* (1.19). In Aetolia Aristomenes remarries. His remarriage points to the 'death' of his former self and thus serves as the last instance of role-changing, brought about through magic within the tale's action. In structural terms, his second marriage at the end of the tale (1.19) forms a structural parallel with the remarriage of Socrates' wife at the tale's opening when her husband was thought to be dead, long before he was actually murdered (1.6).

Aristomenes' lasting punishment beyond the loss of his friend is self-imposed exile. Even then, however, he manages to re-establish a family, in stark contrast to Socrates, who suffers both the loss of his own family and his life. Moreover, Aristomenes' exile also establishes a distant contrast with the sponge: as a human Aristomenes is entitled to free will once Socrates is dead and magic ceases to control him, whereas the inanimate sponge has inevitably returned to the sea.

On the level of the tale's delivery, Aristomenes' previous failure to comprehend events is mirrored in his failure as narrator to persuade his internal audience of fellow travelers as to the truth of his account. At the end of the tale, Aristomenes' unnamed companion again expresses disbelief in the story and then seeks to learn Lucius' opinion, since the latter seems to be an educated man. In response, Lucius reveals his credulity by reasserting his belief in the tale and expressing gratitude and pleasure in hearing it. Lucius' behavior vis-à-vis magic seems to be rather sponge-like: he blindly and eagerly absorbs anything on the subject to the point where he ends up being no more than a 'vessel' for it. He thus makes clear his complete failure to learn anything from Aristomenes' tale of magic. In contrast to the internal audience, readers of the tale may view Aristomenes as unwittingly collaborating in the murder of his friend because of the intervention of magic which he fails to comprehend. The variety of responses to the tale by its distinct auditors reveals the varying reactions the narrative of the *Metamorphoses* may receive from its multiple audiences. In retrospect, the inability of humans to understand the dangers of magic and counteract its effects explains Isis' intervention in the final book of the work, so as to assist Lucius in shedding his asinine form, a direct consequence of his own curiosity regarding magic.

Upon their arrival at the city gates of Hypata, the characters' paths diverge: the two fellow travelers turn to the left to some neighboring villages, while Lucius stops at the first inn to ask for directions to his host Milo's house.

2. Mutilation as Emasculation: Thelyphron's Tale of Thelyphron

Lucius patently fails to draw any lessons about magic from the cautionary tale related by Aristomenes on the road to Hypata. In the town itself he is given the chance to hear yet another such tale, this time at a banquet held by his aunt Byrrhene. The hostess calls upon Thelyphron to narrate the story of his mutilation by witches, in order to entertain her guests and thus offer an indirect warning to her nephew about the dangers of magic. In an earlier sequence (2.5), Byrrhene specifically advised Lucius to avoid Milo's wife Pamphile, another powerful witch, the implication being that anyone ensnared by her love is destined to suffer a fate similar to that of Socrates. Lucius takes his aunt's advice and steers clear of Pamphile, choosing instead to gain access to magic through involvement in an affair with Pamphile's slave Fotis, who is also a witch. The etymology of the names of both Lucius and Fotis suggests their interconnection: the former derives from the Latin term *lux*, meaning light,[50] while the latter comes from the Greek *fotis*, meaning small light.[51] In spite of the fact that Lucius is of noble birth and Fotis is a lowly slave, their affair may be interpreted as a form of 'marriage.' This relationship, however, proves to be fatal as it brings about the protagonist's metamorphosis into an ass and his subsequent misadventures.

In the Thelyphron tale (2.21-30), a widow concocts a scheme to guard the corpse of her young husband from mutilation by witches during the pre-funeral vigil, thereby concealing the fact that she has poisoned him for the sake of her adulterer. Thelyphron agrees to act as guard, but by neglecting his duties he unwittingly takes the place of the dead husband and is punished in his place. The mutilation of Thelyphron mirrors the emasculation of the young husband poisoned by his wife for the sake of her adulterer. Moreover, the witches who put the guard to sleep (a symbolic death) and then mutilate the wrong 'corpse' appear as doubles to the widow who murdered her husband. In taking parts from the wrong corpse, the witches assist the widow in the temporary triumph of her scheme and can thus be viewed as her helpers.[52] Yet whatever the similarities between the dead husband

---

[50] Forcellini 1965, vol. VI, 143 (s.v. *Lucius*).
[51] Forcellini 1965, vol. VI, 486 (s.v. *Photis*).
[52] Cf. Schlam 1992, 70, who observes that "[t]he wife has practiced no magic, but she shows the lust and malevolence of the witches."

and Thelyphron may be, there is one major difference: the former is unwittingly deceived, whereas the latter is fully aware of the dangers of his role. In this way, the tale directs attention to Thelyphron's foolishness in agreeing to take on the challenge of magic in exchange for apparently easy money; his decision to act as guard marks him for life.

Scholars have interpreted the tale of Thelyphron either as a careless *contaminatio* of three independent stories—a tale of witches, a scene of necromancy and an adultery tale[53]—or as an *exemplum* of the laws of causality breaking down, as the witches unexpectedly change their strategy and take parts from the wrong 'corpse.'[54] Others have drawn attention to the affiliations of this tale with the earlier tale of Aristomenes.[55] Still others have noted the switch of roles between guard and dead husband towards the end.[56] The constant role shifting throughout the tale has received little comment, despite the fact that it is a salient feature involving several characters. In what follows I shall focus on this aspect of the narrative, for it reveals the tale's logical coherence and further helps provide unity in the story, which is commonly held to be composed of three independent stories.[57]

---

[53] Perry 1967, 264-73. See also Meyrhofer 1975, 75-80. James 1987, 76-79, considers the lengthening of Thelyphron's story as far from arbitrary, but does not offer further explanation.

[54] Shumate 1996 (a), 81. See also Shumate 1999, 114. Schlam 1992, 70, interprets the tale's *contaminatio* as "evidence of one of the ways thematic structure is established in the work."

[55] Walsh 1970, 153-54.

[56] Winkler 1985, 113-14.

[57] A concise discussion of narratology appears in Hijmans Jr. *et al.* 1995, 7-12. For a brilliant narratological reading of the tale and the interplay between

In the course of Byrrhene's banquet, her nephew Lucius expresses terror regarding rumors he has heard, to the effect that in Thessaly witches remove body parts from the dead to harm the living. One of the guests then points out that even the living are not exempt from punishment. Upon hearing this the guests burst into uproarious laughter and turn to look at Thelyphron, who is sitting in the corner (2.20). The fact that this character is presented as sitting at a distance from the other guests reflects his social isolation on account of facial deformity, while the laughter at his expense reduces him to a piteous spectacle. The disfigured man is offended by the audience's laughter and prepares to leave, but Byrrhene encourages him to stay, tell his tale and thus implicitly instruct her nephew about the dangers of magic. Thelyphron's unwillingness to narrate the tale of his mutilation by witches evokes both Aristomenes and Socrates in the tale of Aristomenes, who were also initially unwilling to narrate their own tale of magic. At the insistence of his hostess, however, Thelyphron takes the proper pose to commence the telling of his tale (2.21):

> [a]c sic aggeratis in cumulum stragulis et effultus in cubitum suberectusque in torum porrigit dexteram et ad instar oratorum conformat articulum duobusque infimis conclusis digitis ceteros eminens et infesto pollice clementer subrigens infit Thelyphron.
>
> And so Thelyphron piled the covers in a heap and propped himself on his elbow, sitting half upright on the couch. He extended his right arm, shaping his fingers to resemble an orator's: having bent his two lowest fingers in, he stretched

---

auctor and *actor*, see Winkler 1985, 110-15. For elements of New Comedy in Apuleius' tale of Cupid and Psyche, see Frangoulidis 1997, 145-177.

the others out at long range and poised his thumb to strike, gently rising as he began.

Here Thelyphron tries to assume the role of storyteller to recount his tale for Byrrhene's guests, and therefore improve his social standing. This description may also be read as an indication of Apuleius' awareness of the performative aspect of the narration of the *Metamorphoses* and, by implication, of Lucius as the principal narrator of the work.

In the tale the young Thelyphron (*pupillus* 2.21; *iuvenis* 2.23) runs out of money on his way to watch the Olympic games. In the forum at Larissa he meets an old man who is looking for someone to guard a corpse against witches who steal bodies during pre-burial vigils. Instead of attending the Olympic games, Thelyphron is thus ironically offered the chance to become a very different kind of spectator. His crucial decision to accept the job results in his transformation into a spectacle on more than one occasion in the narrative.[58]

On Thelyphron's request the old man explains the nature of the job as well as the dangers it involves (2.22):

> 'iam primum,' respondit ille, 'perpetem noctem eximie vigilandum est exertis et inconivis oculis semper in cadaver intentis nec acies usquam devertenda, immo ne obliquanda quidem, quippe cum deterrimae versipelles in quodvis animal ore converso latenter adrepant, ut ipsos etiam oculos Solis et Iustitiae facile frustrentur; nam et aves et rursum

---

[58] In intratextual terms, Thelyphron, whose horrible experience begins on the way to the Olympic games, recalls Aristomenes (Book 1) whose worst misfortune takes place on the way to a gladiatorial spectacle near Larissa. On this parallel, see Scobie 1978, 52. An additional element may be the fact that more than one witch intervenes in both tales.

canes et mures, immo vero etiam muscas induunt. tunc diris cantaminibus somno custodes obruunt. nec satis quisquam definire poterit, quantas latebras nequissimae mulieres pro libidine sua comminiscuntur. nec tamen huius tam exitiabilis operae merces amplior quam quaterni vel seni fermae offeruntur aurei. ehem, et, quod paene praeterieram, siqui non integrum corpus mane restituerit, quidquid inde decerptum deminutumque fuerit, id omne de facie sua desecto sarcire compellitur.'

'First of all,' he replied, 'you must stay perfectly wide awake all night long, with straining unblinking eyes concentrated continuously on the corpse. You must never look around you, or even look aside, because those horrible creatures can change their skins and creep in secretly with their looks transformed into any sort of animal at all. They could easily cheat even the Sun's eyes, or Justice's. They put on the form of birds, and again dogs, and mice—yes, and even flies. Then with their dreadful spells they overwhelm watchmen with sleep. No one can even count the number of subterfuges these evil women contrive on behalf of their lust. And yet, as pay for such dangerous work no more than four or maybe six pieces of gold are offered. Oh yes, and I had almost forgotten to mention that if someone fails to deliver the body unscathed in the morning, he is forced to patch any part that has been plucked off or reduced in size with a piece sliced from his own face.'

Here the old man explains that the witches transform themselves into various animals and insects in order to deceive guards and take parts from corpses for their use. In intratextual terms the old man resembles Byrrhene; he warns Thelyphron in no uncertain terms of the dangers of magic, while Byrrhene's insistence that the tale be told indirectly alerts Lucius to the same issue. The old man's speech functions as an aside, as it reveals the mission as illusionary dangerous. However, Thelyphron foolishly overestimates his abilities, describing himself as more keen-sighted than the mythic Lynceus and Argus. The earlier reference to his lack of money is designed to explain his willingness to watch over the corpse. In narratological terms, the old man's speech may be defined as a 'contract' to be honored by whoever agrees to act as guard. Thelyphron is then led to the house of the deceased and introduced to a *matrona*, dressed in black and wailing loudly over the loss of her husband. As narrator Thelyphron relates his subsequent introduction by the old man to the widow, and the ensuing exchange between the widow and himself regarding the demands of his role (2.23).

In the actantial structure, the arrangement of actors/characters may appear as follows: the widow fills the position of the sender, while Thelyphron appears in the place of the subject, the object being to guard the corpse. The witches seemingly appear in the position of the opponent, but in fact turn out to be the widow's helpers, since they take parts from the wrong 'dead man.' Finally, the old man who introduces Thelyphron to the widow also fills the helper's place, as he assists her in finding a guard.

In his exchange with the widow, Thelyphron makes a most unfitting aside on her beauty (2.23): *at illa crinibus antependulis hinc inde dimotis etiam in maerore luculentam proferens faciem*. This comment reveals Thelyphron's interest in the widow and thus makes him remotely equivalent to her dead husband, a fact which may help to explain the later exchange of roles between the guard and the deceased, with the resultant punishment of the former rather than the latter.

After their conversation the widow takes Thelyphron to the next room, mourns her husband for a while and shows him the corpse in the presence of seven witnesses (2.24): *'ecce,' inquit, 'nasus integer, incolumes oculi, salvae aures, inlibatae labiae, mentum solidum.'* The emphasis in this section falls on external body parts, because they are easily recognizable if missing. The presence of the witnesses in the room is designed to maintain the illusion of the widow as a faithful wife. These attendants will later confirm the fulfillment of the 'contract' by the guard, as the old man has explained to him (2.22). Before the widow's departure, Thelyphron asks her for a lamp with oil, plenty of wine and a dinner platter (2.24): *'[l]ucerna,' aio, 'praegrandis et oleum ad lucem luci sufficiens et calida cum oenophoris et calice cenarumque reliquiis discus ornatus.'* Thelyphron's request for abundant food and wine reveals his inability to understand the dangers of his job as well as the seriousness of the situation; rather than staying alert, he seeks to recreate the atmosphere of a banquet. Furthermore, his reference to leftovers from dinner may suggest that the widow is having a feast at the time of mourning. All the same, she wishes to play out the role of bereaved spouse and thus orders the guard to assume a suitably mournful posture (2.24): *'quin sumis potius loco congruentes luctus et lacrimas?'* She further instructs her attendant Myrrhine to give the guard nothing more than a lamp and lock him up in the same room as the deceased. In spatial terms the widow's orders can be seen as highlighting the interconnection between guard and deceased husband in their common role as rejected mates.

In the performance proper during the night, Thelyphron deviates from the demands of his role: first he tries to stay awake by singing, then he forgets that witches can assume the form of

Unwittingly Successful Performances: The Triumph of Magic

various animals, and so mistakes the witch who enters the room for a weasel, urging it to go away (2.25). The creature withdraws, but soon Thelyphron falls into a deep sleep, which he identifies as a descent into the underworld (2.25):

> somnus profundus in imum barathrum repente demergit, ut ne deus quidem Delficus ipse facile discerneret duobus nobis iacentibus, quis esset magis mortuus.
>
> Instantly deep slumber plunged me swiftly down to the bottom of the abyss. Even the god of Delphi could not easily have decided which of the two of us lying there was more dead.

In the above passage, Thelyphron's self-characterization as deceased establishes an interconnection between him and the corpse. His ensuing reference to his own need for a guard, *indigens alio custode* (2.25), because of his sleep—symbolically represented as death—foreshadows the resurrection of the widow's husband the next day to recount how his guard came to be horribly mutilated by the witches during the vigil (2.30). Both men have doubled for each other.

In the morning Thelyphron awakes and observes that the corpse is unmutilated, but fails to realize that he himself has fallen victim to magic. The widow then re-enters the room in tears, accompanied by the same witnesses as on the previous night. Having examined the corpse, she orders the payment of her guard and informs him that she will consider him a member of her family. Thelyphron rejoins by asking her to bear him in mind for future occasions (2.26): '*et quotiens operam nostram desiderabis, fidenter impera.*' Winkler interprets this reply in the context of *savoir vivre*: he observes that the widow is offered services "for the corpses of all her future husbands."[59] However, the term *opera* is also used in the same way as the term *opus*, suggesting "the male part in the act."[60] In this context, the reply helps to characterize Thelyphron as the widow's would-be lover, and thus, in some sense, as analogous to her dead husband. This equivocal use of the term *opera* counters the widow's role as a faithful wife. Her attendants, who seem to be aware of her scheme, beat Thelyphron and throw him out of the house, thus signaling the abrupt end of his role as guard. This development strikes yet another parallel with the dead husband, who is taken out of the *same* room for burial immediately afterwards.

The whole conspiracy is finally unmasked in the open space of the forum. As the funeral procession enters, a genuinely grief-stricken mourner accuses the widow of poisoning his nephew for the sake of her lover. The forum is the very same civic space where the old man hired Thelyphron the previous day. The plausibility of the bereaved uncle's accusations angers the crowd, who demand the widow be severely punished (2.27): *conclamant ignem, requirunt saxa, parent lora ad exitium mulieris hortantur.*[61] In his capacity as narrator Thelyphron also mentions the widow's crocodile tears (*emenditatis ... fletibus* 2.27), but fails to realize that he has doubled for her deceased husband in her scheme. The widow's impassioned denial of the accusations forces the elderly uncle to appeal to the

---

[59] Winkler 1985, 111.
[60] Adams 1982, 157, lists this Apuleian passage.
[61] The reaction of the crowd forms a thematic parallel with the widow's attendants, who had previously beaten the guard when he made his inopportune comment on the widow's mores.

Egyptian prophet Zatchlas, and offer him a large fee to revive the dead man for as long as it takes to prove the widow's guilt.[62]

The uncle's appeal to the priest can be viewed as a further plan. The theatrical aspect of this necromantic ritual also becomes clear from the use of the term *scaena* (2.28), which points to the language of theater.[63] In this plan, the position of all actors/characters in the actantial structure is transformed as follows: in hiring the priest, the aged uncle assumes the position of the widow who had earlier hired the guard; the priest takes the place of the subject, which was earlier reserved for the guard. The goal/value is in this case to reanimate the corpse and thus provide indubitable evidence regarding the circumstances of his death. Thelyphron and the crowd fill the position of the helper, originally occupied by the widow's witnesses, but with precisely the opposite aim: they are there to prove her guilt rather than her innocence. This shift of the actors'/characters' position in the actantial structure also points to a 'revision' of the larger tale.

In the execution of his role, the priest carries out the religious part of the ceremony and revives the dead man, but the latter expresses his unwillingness to return to life (2.29):[64]

---

[62] van Mal-Maeder 1997, 100, discusses the awkward feature of the priest's offering his services at a fee. On the basis of this and other evidence van Mal-Maeder establishes a connection between Isis and the witches. Moreover, like the young Thelyphron (*pupillus* 2.21; *iuvenis* 2.23), the priest is also portrayed as young (*iuvenis* 2.28). There is a major contrast though: the priest controls magic (necromancy), while Thelyphron is the victim of it.

[63] *OLD*, s.v. *scaena* 5, cites this passage and translates it "a piece of artificial or melodramatic behavior designed to impress, 'charade,' 'theatricals'."

[64] Graverini 1998, 132-33, develops an association between Zatchlas and the Sibyl in Vergil's *Aeneid* 6.

'[q]uid, oro, me post Lethaea pocula iam Stygiis paludibus innatantem ad momentariae vitae reducitis officia? desine iam, precor, desine, ac me in meam quietem permitte.'

'Why,' he asked, 'when after Lethe's draughts I was already swimming in the Stygian pool, why are you bringing me back to the functions of life for but a moment? Stop now, I beg you. Stop and let me go back to my rest.'

The image of the revived husband crossing the Styx evokes the guard who had earlier described his sleep as a descent into the underworld (2.25). The dead husband is unwilling to speak, thereby focusing attention on the import of his testimony. At this point the priest emphasizes his authority over the powers of death and thus forces him to speak (2.29).

The corpse then rises from the bier in his burial 'costume' and confirms every detail of the accusations made by his uncle. The widow denies everything yet again, but the husband points to his guard and reveals the illusion of the events which took place during the vigil. It transpires that the guard mistakenly answered the witches' call to the dead because they had poured a death-like sleep over him. The witches then cut off the guard's nose and ears and replaced them with false ones made of wax, so as to conceal their evil magic (2.30).

In the actantial structure guard and dead husband switch positions during the vigil: the guard assumes the object position, and what was previously the object becomes the subject (2.25).[65] This displacement is facilitated by the fact that both guard and

---

[65] Winkler 1985, 113-14, discusses this reversal of narrator and narrated (Thelyphron for Thelyphron) in the tale, while Dowden 1998, 12, observes that "you are safe from witches when you are awake."

dead husband have the same name, Thelyphron. Furthermore, the witches end up as the widow's helpers rather than her opponents; in taking body parts from the 'wrong' dead man, they assist in the temporary triumph of her scheme. In the aged uncle's plan the widow cannot maintain her role as chaste wife, and thus both her scheme and crime are exposed.[66]

The punishment of the guard mirrors the fate suffered by the dead husband in several ways. Firstly, mutilation points to the loss of the guard's male sexual identity, since he is left so ugly that no woman will ever fall in love with him again. From a Freudian perspective, the mutilation of extremities (in the context of marriage, adultery, courtship, etc.) is considered to have sexual overtones.[67] The guard's facial deformity evokes the husband's loss of manhood, as reflected by the correlation of the following contextual elements: (a) the unmanly manner of his death (poisoning at the hands of his spouse); and (b) the wife's involvement in an affair with an adulterer.[68] Secondly, just as the guard discovers his mutilation after his adventure with the witches,

---

[66] Structurally, Zatchlas' act contrasts with that of the witches from every perspective: (1) The priest reanimates the dead husband in order to expose the widow's crime, in contrast to the witches, who put the guard into a death-like sleep and then remove parts from his face (see also Tatum 1969, 501; and van Mal-Maeder 1997, 99-100). (2) Zatchlas performs his rite in the open space of the forum during daytime, thus counterbalancing the witches, who have earlier performed their magical rites in the inner space of a dark room at midnight. (3) The priest reanimates the deceased for a certain period of time, in contrast to the witches, who mark the guard forever in life.

[67] Adams 1982, 35, points out that the term *nasus* often serves as metaphor for the male sexual organ.

[68] Cf. Ingenkamp 1972, 337-42, who interprets Thelyphron's loss of his ears and nose as the punishment of an adulterer. For a similar view see also Graverini 1998, 129-131.

so the husband acquires an understanding of his wife's sexual mores only after his death. Thirdly, the guard has the same name as the dead husband, Thelyphron, which derives from the Greek term *theluphron*, meaning 'effeminate,'[69] and hence effectively brings out the gender problem in the identity of both guard and dead husband—a consequence of their adventures with the same woman. Finally, the synonymy of the guard and the dead husband is concealed in the narrative until it no longer endangers the widow's scheme, only to be disclosed after both men have suffered humiliation by the same woman.

In his astonishment, foolish Thelyphron confirms the veracity of the husband's story: he touches his nose and ears and discovers that they are indeed made of wax and come off. On a symbolic level the guard's unmasking also signals the end of the illusion. The watching crowd bursts into uproarious laughter as they point and nod at the noseless and earless Thelyphron. Having been an observer of the priest's miracle, he is transformed once more into a spectacle. The shame caused by the mutilation is so great that Thelyphron does not return to his home in Miletus, just as Aristomenes relocates to Aitolia, thus illustrating that victims of magic cannot go home. Instead Thelyphron grows his hair and covers his nose with a linen bandage, putting on another 'mask' in order to cover-up his deformed face. This final instance of role-metamorphosis brought about through magic brings the tale full circle, for it is in this same role that Thelyphron first appears in the narrative.

---

[69] See van Mal-Maeder 1998, 293; also Kenney 1998, 226, translates the term as 'womanheart.'

Unwittingly Successful Performances: The Triumph of Magic

The witches who put the guard into a death-like sleep and then symbolically emasculate him appear in an analogous position to the widow, whose actions indirectly deprive her husband of his manhood. The guard's full knowledge of the dangers involved in his job set him apart from the husband, even though both suffer what amounts to the same punishment. Hence the tale reveals the disastrous effects of carelessly coming into contact with magic.

Yet again, Lucius fails to heed the warnings that the tale eloquently illustrates. His failure is all the more acute when one considers the motivation behind his earlier ill-thought decision to involve himself in an affair with Fotis. As we know, this will later lead to his metamorphosis into an ass. In this sense, the rich pattern of role changes helps to dispel the logical inconsistencies within the narrative, while simultaneously placing Thelyphron's tale within the context of Lucius' wider experiences in the novel.

3. The Laughter Festival as a Community Integration Rite

In 2.32 Lucius returns late at night from Byrrhene's dinner-party to Milo's house, accompanied by his slave. In his drunken state he sees what he thinks are three robbers trying to break into Milo's house, and kills them one by one with his sword. The following morning Lucius weeps as he envisages his likely prosecution for the murders. There is a marked contrast between this hung-over remorse and the drunken bravado of the previous night.[70] The protagonist's differing perceptions of the same event

---

[70] Penwill *per litteras*.

may be defined as plots. The Hypatans take advantage of Lucius' pessimistic scenario and stage a mock trial, during the course of which Lucius acts out two roles: the accused criminal and the orator, defending the heroism of his deed. These admirably correspond to the two distinct plots and tie in neatly with the key theme of metamorphosis.

Lucius' unwitting performance in the festival acquires the ritual function of *dokimasia* in rites of passage. Lucius is an outsider and the Hypatans offer him the splendid opportunity of staying in their town by testing his abilities to generate laughter. Although Lucius passes the test and the Hypatans make him patron of their city, offering to cast his image in bronze, he turns down these high honors. The refusal to integrate into the Hypatan community on Lucius' part may be explained by the fact that their Laughter god has offered him sorrow instead of joy. What is more remarkable is that Lucius fails to comprehend the role of witchcraft in his misfortunes during the Laughter festival. Shortly afterwards, this unshaken overconfidence with regard to magic leads to his transformation into an ass. The group of robbers who break into Milo's house and carry him away with the loot to their mountain den marks the beginning of his sorrowful adventures. In these adventures, Lucius as ass is a victim of ridicule—the narrative of his subsequent adventures mirrors his earlier ordeal in the Laughter festival.

Unwittingly Successful Performances: The Triumph of Magic

Scholars have traditionally interpreted the Laughter festival as a scapegoat ritual.[71] Habinek offers the most illuminating discussion in this regard, but interprets the festival as a rite of communal identity in which Lucius plays the *pharmakos*—a marginal figure, whose presence in the town threatens harmony, so that his expulsion ensures communal identity.[72] Others have pointed out the theatrical substructure of the narrative,[73] in some cases defining Lucius' experience in the festival as a replay of the misadventures previously suffered by Aristomenes and Thelyphron.[74]

My aim in what follows is to counter the view that Lucius acts as a scapegoat figure in the Laughter festival. Instead I will argue that the narrative of *Met.* 3.1-12 represents an integration ritual, in which Lucius and all other participants engage in role-playing. That being said, there is a major difference between Lucius and all other characters: the former acts unwittingly, while the latter are conscious of their roles.

After the end of Thelyphron's tale, Byrrhene informs Lucius that the Laughter festival is due to take place the following day, and advises him to find something witty to celebrate this great god (2.31). Lucius promises to do his best, leaving the house in a drunken state. Upon his arrival at Milo's house, he sees three 'men,'

---

[71] James 1987, 87 and 97, n. 1; and McCreight 1993, 46-47. On the other hand, Robertson 1919, 110-15, interprets the festival as a ritual drama of the carnival type.

[72] Habinek 1990, 54; Bartalucci 1988, 50-65; Finkelpearl 1998, 91-92, compares Lucius with Sinon in Vergil's *Aeneid* 2 in their common role of scapegoats. For the ritual of *pharmakos* see Burkert 1985, 82-84.

[73] Penwill 1990, 5.

[74] Tatum 1979, 49. The point is made but not developed any further.

whom he mistakes for robbers beating on the door, and kills them one by one with his sword. These 'robbers' later turn out to have been wineskins animated by Pamphile's magic. As narrator, Lucius compares his encounter with these bandits to that of Hercules' slaughtering of Geryon: *in vicem Geryoneae* (2.32).

In the actantial model, Lucius fills the position of the subject whose object/value is to kill three would-be burglars entering his host's home. Through his actions Lucius hopes to protect Milo's property and thus reveal his noble character. The 'robbers' occupy the place of the opponent and the slave Fotis acts as the helper. Fotis hears the noise and opens the door. Lucius enters the house still sweating and then goes to sleep after his epic fight. From a theatrical perspective, the representation of wineskins as valiant men may be interpreted as yet another mask or role.

On the morning of the Laughter festival, the Hypatans take advantage of the protagonist's guilty conscience and put him on a mock trial, charging him with triple 'murder.' The farce is staged on the premise that as a common criminal, Lucius must undergo a ritual 'catharsis' before he can be integrated into the Hypatan community and join their 'fellowship of Laughter.'

In the narrative of the Laughter festival, there are clearly two distinct actantial structures, one from the perspective of the Hypatans, who plan to honor the god of Laughter, and one from the perspective Lucius trying to acquit himself from murder charges. It is the difference in the object of these two structures that creates tension in the narrative.

More specifically, in the Hypatans' plan to celebrate the Laughter festival, the distribution of characters may be arranged as follows: the god of Laughter and the Hypatan community (literally here, as they send men to arrest Lucius) appear in the position of the sender. In this plan Lucius is the unwitting subject. The object is to create mirth and thus honor the god of Laughter. Both the Hypatan community and Lucius, who is to be accepted as a member in the community, fill the receiver position. The wineskins, the witnesses, the prosecution and Lucius in both roles as accused and council for the defense occupy the helper's place. The opponent's position is left vacant, although it may be filled by Lucius if he fails to act out his part well.

In his plan to acquit himself, Lucius occupies the position of both the sender and receiver, while also appearing in the subject position in his roles as criminal and defendant. His object is to acquit himself in the ensuing 'trial.' The Hypatans in their role as prosecutors and witnesses fill the opponent position, along with the wineskins, since they are presented as the main trial evidence. In this structure there is no external helper other than Lucius.

The complete lack of historical evidence relating to Laughter festivals[75] bears out Byrrhene's earlier remark to Lucius that the Hypatans are the only people in the world who celebrate this rite: *quo die soli mortalium sanctissimum deum Risum hilaro atque gaudiali ritu propitiamus* (2.31). However, the narrative in question may offer some useful insights into the motivation for the festival. It appears to be an institutionalized ritual of integration in which the entire community participates, thus symbolizing its cohesion as a group. The entire procedure seems to involve some sort of a mock trial, the literal equivalent of *dokimasia* that informs rites of passage. The Hypatans seem to prefer setting up either strangers or fools (ideally

---

[75] See Schlam 1992, 43.

both, like Lucius), because such people are ignorant of the rite and can thus ensure a triumphant celebration for Laughter.

The performance of the trial begins when the magistrates, the lictors and a mob of citizens burst into Milo's house, arrest Lucius and take him to court to face murder charges. Lucius surrenders to the lictors without offering any resistance, thus implicitly acquiescing to the role of criminal as he is led around the town: *lustralibus ... hostiis* 3.2 (also a few lines later: *velut quandam victimam* 3.2).[76]

Intratextually, Lucius' misguided remorse at murdering three 'citizens' the following morning could be compared with that of Aristomenes, who is convinced that Socrates' murder the previous night was all a bad dream. Unlike Aristomenes, however, who interprets the crime committed by the witches as a bad dream, Lucius is convinced that an essentially farcical event of no import was a true murder. He is thus transformed from a drunken carouser full of courage into a cowardly object of merriment in the festival. Moreover, Lucius' misguided remorse at murdering three citizens could be viewed as a mirror image of Aristomenes' guilt at not having prevented his friend's murder. In such a schema, however, Aristomenes emerges more favorably, because his involvement in magic was motivated by an unselfish wish to act as a true friend of Socrates (unless one takes Socrates' initial reticence to be a covert warning), unlike the noble Lucius, who has no justification whatsoever for getting involved in magic other than ego-driven curiosity.

---

[76] For the sacrificial language in the Laughter festival, see McCreight 1993, 46-52.

Unwittingly Successful Performances: The Triumph of Magic

The fact that Lucius likens himself to an animal has been taken by some scholars as evidence for his role as *pharmakos*.[77] Although this reading is in alignment with Lucius' own interpretation of events, it is also possible to interpret the animal imagery as foreshadowing his imminent metamorphosis into an ass and his subsequent misadventures. The ridicule he suffers both at the festival and thereafter is a direct result of his foolhardy interest in magic.

Moreover, in his capacity as narrator Lucius describes the entire crowd as laughing at him throughout the procession to the place of trial. This laughter suggests enjoyment and approval of the protagonist's performance, given that the Hypatans are aware of his innocence.[78]

When the procession reaches the forum shortly afterwards, the magistrates take their seat in the lofty tribunal, *sublimo suggestu*, and thus assume the role of *judices*, judges (3.2). On account of overcrowding the procedure is moved to the theater, as there is serious danger of a genuine disaster, which would be most unfitting at a Laughter festival. At the same time, the locale of the theater serves as the most appropriate setting for the enactment of this 'staged' trial. Lucius emerges as all the more stupid for failing to take note of this change of venue. After all, his aunt has already informed him about the festival and hinted that he will be called upon to play a role.

---

[77] Bartalucci 1988, 58; also Robertson 1919, 113-14.

[78] For an assessment of the (sadistic) laughter in the festival, see Shumate 1996 (a), 83-86.

In the performance proper, the crier calls for silence and asks the watchman to come forward to deliver his speech. A water-clock is used to time the speech and thus maintain the illusion of an actual trial. The watchman assumes the role of prosecutor, *accusator* (3.3), and delivers the accusation in accordance with the form prescribed in rhetorical textbooks: an *exordium* (3.3.2-3), a *narratio* (3.3.4-8) and a *peroratio* (3.3.9).[79]

In the *exordium*, the prosecutor points out the importance of the case and asks for the punishment of the murderer. He emphasizes the eye-witness nature of his account in order to lend authority to his narrative. The *narratio* relates the facts of the case. The previous night, the defendant is alleged to have killed three men and then entered a house. The prosecutor dutifully made sure to bring him to justice the next day, which coincided with the holiday. On such occasions the courts are only ever convened if some serious crime affecting the entire community is to be tried.[80] The early sections of the speech serve to shed light on the events that have taken place between the previous night and the trial itself.[81] In the *peroratio*, the prosecutor appeals to the judges to punish the murderer, whom he characterizes as *peregrinus*, foreigner. This punishment would take the form of expulsion from the town (as in 10.12, when the wicked stepmother is expelled

---

[79] van der Paardt 1971, 47. The reference to the text is to the Budé edition of Robertson and Vallette 1940-45.

[80] See Geffcken 1973, 12, on Caelius' trial on the day of the *Ludi Megalenses* (April 4, 56 BCE) in Cicero's *Pro Caelio*.

[81] For this difficulty, see van der Paardt 1971, 3-6.

from town for plotting to poison her stepson).[82] The fact that Lucius plays the part of defendant in the festival, albeit unwittingly, offers him a rare opportunity to integrate into the community and attain the status of an honorary citizen. Everything depends on his skill in generating laughter, thereby assisting in the festival celebrations in honor of the god.[83] As we said earlier, Lucius must undergo the ritual 'catharsis' provided by the trial before he can be fully accepted into the Hypatan community as one of its members.

The crier then calls upon the accused to defend himself. Lucius bursts into tears, not so much because of the accusation, but out of his own foolish sense of guilt. Still, he musters some courage, which he attributes to divine inspiration, and presents his case in terms of the heroic nature of his deed (3.4).

Finkelpearl has recently interpreted Lucius' defense in the trial as evidence for his dual role as *auctor* and *actor*. Lucius creates a speech and proceeds to deliver it to the audience at the trial.[84] His role as *auctor*, however, may be more clearly illustrated by the two plots he unknowingly devises the night before the festival and the following morning. In so doing he is subtly fulfilling his promise to his aunt to find something witty with which to celebrate the god of Laughter. During the festival, Lucius executes both roles first as criminal and then as defendant, trying to prove his innocence in

---

[82] James 1987, 88-89, observes a contrast between the Hypatans who treat the foreigner Lucius with suspicion, and the magistrates who offer him a dedicatory statue.

[83] One may further recall Fotis' earlier remark in 2.18 that the Hypatans are hostile to foreigners perhaps because they prefer to set them up in the festival and thus ensure its success: *'tibi vero fortunae splendor insidias, contemptus etiam peregrinationis poterit adferre.'*

[84] Finkelpearl 1998, 89.

the performance of the 'trial.' Moreover, his defense in the 'trial' exhibits a rhetorical structure, consisting of an *exordium* (3.4.3-4), a *narratio* (3.5-6.1-3) and a section of *proofs* (3.6.4-5), just like the watchman's speech before it.[85]

In the *exordium* Lucius does not deny the charge of murdering three men. After all, the biers are present in the orchestra. Instead he argues that the accusation against him is unreasonable. In this way, Lucius uses emotional appeal to arouse sympathy in his audience for his poor plight. In the *narratio*, he relates the facts of the case as he wants them to be understood by his audience. The previous night, Lucius had seen three robbers trying to break down Milo's door and kill those inside the house (he even quotes the exhortation of the leader verbatim to enhance the verisimilitude of his account). When he tried to force these robbers to flee, their ringleader attacked him. Lucius represents this encounter as a duel, thus lending an epic dimension to the scene. This recalls his earlier representation of his deeds the night before the 'trial' (*in vicem Geryoneae* 2.32). Lucius struck down the robber and killed the other two with his sword. In this way, he protected Milo's house from robbery and restored public order. For this reason, he views himself as worthy of public praise: *salute communi protecta ... me ... laudabilem publice credebam fore* (3.6). In retrospect, the people of Hypata praise Lucius not for ridding society of criminals, but for his skill in generating laughter in the festival and hence duly honoring the god of Laughter. In the closing section of his speech, Lucius refers to the esteem in which

---

[85] van der Paardt 1971, 64. The reference to the text is to the Budé edition of Robertson and Vallette 1940-45.

Unwittingly Successful Performances: The Triumph of Magic

he is held among his own people as well as to the absence of any motive for committing the crime.

After his defense Lucius weeps once more. When he is sure that he has won over the audience, he stares at them, but discovers to his amazement that everyone including his host has dissolved into laughter.[86] At this point Lucius blames Milo for ingratitude. One way of interpreting Milo's response is as that of an informed spectator: he is aware of the positive development that awaits his guest, and is thus free to enjoy the excellent performance in the 'trial.'[87]

At this point two women appear in the orchestra. One is a young mother holding a child in her arms, the other is decidedly older (3.8). These women act out the roles of the widows and mothers of the dead men respectively. The reference to their black dress must be interpreted as 'costume.' In their turn they deliver an emotional appeal to the court, seeking the defendant's blood (whom they identify as *latro*, robber) in order to placate the dead (3.8). As we would expect in this staged trial, their appeal is successful. The elder of the magistrates (another actor in this 'trial' plot) orders that Lucius be severely tortured in order to reveal the identity of his accomplices; he could not have committed such a crime by himself, yet his slave had escaped. Lucius undergoes the worst kind of humiliation, taking the place of his slave and facing the prospect of corporal punishment, which was forbidden for

---

[86] Penwill 1990, 3, observes the error of the Hypatans as they ignore the role of magic in the animated wineskins. See also Finkelpearl 1998, 90.

[87] Shumate 1996 (a), 87, views Milo both as a trickster figure who laughs at Lucius' expense, and as Lucius' only friend in the crowd. Smith 1989, 130, characterizes Milo as "an ominous and disturbing character."

Roman citizens, let alone nobles of his stature. At this point the older woman appeals to the citizens to pull off the shroud over the corpses, on the grounds that the horrific sight beneath will lead them to call for an even more severe punishment. Lucius' refusal to lay the 'corpses' bare reveals his unwillingness to gaze on the havoc he wrought the previous night. He further describes his experience as a descent into the realm of the dead. Under pressure from the lictors, Lucius removes the shroud, only to discover that his 'victims' were actually wineskins, pierced in the place where he struck them the night before with his sword. It is only then that he fully perceives the illusion of events.

The audience respond with uncontrolled laughter and congratulate Lucius for his performance as they exit the theater. Their laughter is more intense at this moment since nobody represses it, signifying their earlier masked assumption of the role as spectators in the performance of this 'trial.'

An intratextual reading recalls the uncontrolled laughter of people in the funeral procession when they witnessed Thelyphron discover the loss of his nose and ears to the witches (2.30). This connection helps characterize Lucius as a fool, no better than the guard Thelyphron before him. When Lucius perceives the illusion of his creation, he portrays himself as figuratively dead, likening himself to a statue or a column in the theater (3.10).[88] His 'rebirth' occurs only when Milo approaches him and leads him home ever inconsolable after his humiliation during the festival.

---

[88] A brilliant discussion of Lucius' immobility and anaesthesia in the theater is to be found in Winkler 1985, 170-71.

Soon the magistrates re-enter Lucius' room in their stately dress, thus signaling the abandonment of their role of *judices* and, therefore, as opponents in the performance of the 'trial.' Their speech performs the function of explaining the rite to him in every perspective (3.11). First, the magistrates reveal their awareness of Lucius' noble birth and learning, while encouraging him to dispel his grief.[89] This reference to the protagonist's origins only serves to stress his foolishness in failing to comprehend that he has fallen victim to a mock trial. Second, the magistrates define this trial as *lusus*, which the entire community celebrates in honor of the god Laughter. They explain that the success of this *lusus* depends on its novelty value, in this way implicitly making a meta-literary comment on the novel aspect of Lucius' two plots. Third, the magistrates assure Lucius that the god always takes the *auctor* and *actor* under his protection, never letting him experience grief (*auctorem et actorem* 3.11). Such an analysis bears a striking similarity to the two distinct roles performed by Lucius: he is first seen as maker of the two plots and then as actor, when he performs his two roles as the accused and the orator in the enactment of the 'trial.'[90] Finally, the magistrates inform Lucius that the city has decreed to proclaim him patron, *patronus*, and to cast his image in bronze (3.11): *'at tibi civitas omnis pro ista gratia honores egregios obtulit; nam et patronum scribsit et ut in aere stet imago tua decrevit.'* [91] The

---

[89] Harrison 2000, 215-19, collects evidence in the text which reveals Lucius as a sophist in the making.

[90] See Finkelpearl 1998, 89.

[91] Kenney 1998, 228, observes: "in the real world *patronus* was a sort of ambassador, a man of substance and influence appointed to watch over the city's interests at Rome. Lucius' appointment, like the statue which he tactfully declines, is purely honorific."

awarding of exceptional honors to Lucius for his brilliant performance in the festival, so alien to the role of *pharmakos*, signals his integration into the Hypatan community with the new social status of 'honorary citizen.'

In his reply Lucius pretends to acknowledge the import of the distinctions conferred upon him, but tactfully declines the offer of a statue, proposing instead to have it cast in the form of his superiors. He argues that he did not do anything special to deserve these honors, in contrast to all those Hypatans who were aware of their roles, and consciously played them out in the re-enactment of the 'trial.' Moreover, a statue would only serve as an eternal reminder of his role as fool in the festival.[92] The fact that Lucius views himself as a victim rather than an honored guest explains his refusal of the exceptional honors conferred.

Lucius has two diametrically opposed experiences in Hypata. As listener of the Thelyphron tale he can join with Byrrhene's guests in laughing at the disfigured man's misfortune, while in the Laughter festival he finds himself in the position of the victim and is reduced to tears. Since he cannot bear to be the victim of a joke, Lucius refuses the offer of integration into the Hypatan community and their 'fellowship of Laughter,' a refusal which is echoed in his ensuing alienation from the community. When Byrrhene extends him a further invitation to her home, he turns it down for fear that he will be laughed at if called upon to narrate his ordeal (3.12), just as Thelyphron before him (2.21-30). When in a later sequence he is forced by Milo to attend the baths, Lucius

---

[92] Winkler 1985, 171. James 1987, 89, suggests that Lucius is punished because he refuses to enter into the spirit of the festival, as represented by the laughter of his worshippers.

walks to one side so as to avoid the sarcastic laughter and gestures of the crowd.

After the trial Lucius' mistress Fotis comes to his room in tears, relates the story of Pamphile's magic and explains her own role in the crime mocked in the Laughter festival. The 'robbers' were wineskins animated by Pamphile's magic. Fearing Pamphile's anger, she substituted the hair of Pamphile's Boeotian lover with goatskin hair. In his drunken state Lucius mistook these animated wineskins for robbers and pierced them with his sword. In the light of this information the Hypatans appear in a comparable position to Lucius, since they too were ignorant of the role of magic in his ordeal.[93] Fotis then points out to Lucius the true mythic analogue to his act: Ajax driven mad and slaughtering sheep (*in insani modum Aiacis armatus* 3.18). Neither Lucius nor Ajax can then bear the shame of what they thought was an act of heroism turning them into figures of ridicule. Fotis does not explain at any point what subsequently happened. Perhaps, as Kenney observes, "the reader is left to infer that the subsequent performance must have been set up by Milo when he discovered what had happened."[94]

In the run up to the Laughter festival Lucius unwittingly comes into contact with magic and suffers greatly as a result.[95] As one would expect, he fails to keep this in mind and offers to pardon Fotis in return for a glimpse of Pamphile's magic. Readers may recall Byrrhene's earlier warning to Lucius to stay away from Pamphile and her wicked arts: *cave fortiter a malis artibus et facinorosis*

---

[93] Eloquently put forward by Penwill 1990, 5.
[94] Kenney 1998, 228.
[95] Schlam 1992, 34.

illecebris Pamphiles illius (2.5). Although Lucius makes a conscious decision to follow this advice, through his relationship with Fotis he does in fact get involved with a witch.

Fotis lets Lucius see Pamphile as she changes into an owl in order to fly to her Boeotian lover. This transformation makes such an impression on the protagonist that he begs his mistress to change him into a bird, so that he too may fly around her, like a winged Cupid around Venus (3.22). Fotis is unwilling to do so, fearing that he will fly away from her, but finally yields when Lucius promises never to desert her. Fotis reveals herself as a completely amateur witch through her inability to distinguish between the magic boxes. The result is that she accidentally changes her lover into an ass instead of a bird (3.24). Thus Lucius' earlier decision to gain access to magic via Fotis proves to be completely misguided and foolish.

The ill-executed metamorphosis can be seen as punishment for both Fotis and Lucius. The former tried to deceive Pamphile by bringing her goat hair rather than human hair, while the latter metaphorically killed Pamphile's lover by piercing the wineskins with his sword.

Inside the ass-hide Lucius is greatly inferior to his former self in terms of appearance: the handsome man turns into an ugly animal.[96] In this unattractive form, the only consolation is the enlargement of his sexual organ. The ass is slow-moving, in ironic contrast to the desire Lucius expressed to become a swift-moving bird.

---

[96] Bradley 2000, 114, eloquently brings out the antitheses between Lucius as a man and as an ass.

Unwittingly Successful Performances: The Triumph of Magic

That being said, even after the transformation Lucius retains certain traits he displayed as a human being; his animal persona mirrors his human character in several ways. First of all, there is his lustfulness as a man. All too obvious in his affair with Fotis, this parallels his sexual appetite as an ass, when he desires the most beautiful mares in the fields to mate with: *ego tandem liber asinus laetus et tripudians graduque molli gestiens equas opportunissimas iam mihi concubinas futuras deligebam* (7.16). Secondly, there is his curiosity as a human, revealed in his naive interest in magic. This is mirrored by his curiosity as an animal, which on one occasion leads him to betray the hiding place of the market gardener: *curiosus alioquin ... asinus* (9.42). Finally, there is his complete and utter failure to heed any warnings about the catastrophic power of magic. This re-emerges when as an ass he sets in motion the events that lead to the death of his dear master, the miller (Book 9). Just as Lucius himself asserts, throughout his asinine adventures he retains his human mind.

Viewed in another way, Lucius' earlier unwitting performance as a laughing stock in the Laughter festival may be seen as a trial of his foolishness; in successfully passing the test, he has earned the right to become an ass. In 10.13 Lucius the ass makes an implicit comment on the foolishness of asses: *nec enim tam stultus eram tamque vere asinus*.

There are several ways in which Lucius' punishment resembles that suffered by Thelyphron. Both characters are ridiculed in front of a crowd because of an initial failure to recognize magic when they come in contact with it: Thelyphron chases away the weasel in his role as an over-zealous guard overcome by sleep, and Lucius 'kills' the wine-skins in an attempt to act the over-zealous 'guard' overcome by wine. In both cases unmasking is done in front of an audience and causes ridicule. Lucius' ensuing punishment, however, differs considerably from that of Thelyphron: Thelyphron loses his ears and nose, symbolizing the loss of his male sexual identity; whereas Lucius changes into a virile but stupid animal (Ch. I.2).

Lucius' metamorphosis into an ass signals the abrupt end of his 'marriage' to the slave Fotis, with whom he never reunites, despite previous assurances to the contrary. This development seems to offer an alternative turn to the standardized plot of Greek romances, in which the beloved couple separate and then go through adventures before their happy reunion at the end of the novel.

Lucius even considers killing Fotis for changing him into an animal, but stops short of doing so, because he realizes this would cost him the roses, the antidote to metamorphosis she promises to bring him the following morning. Lucius the ass then withdraws overnight to Milo's stable to await the roses, thus signaling his separation from Fotis. At the very least this indicates the temporary acceptance of his new role as an animal, which is not one Lucius chooses for himself, but rather one imposed on him through metamorphosis.

In the nighttime sequence that follows, a group of robbers break into Milo's house, load up the ass and various other animals with their loot and head off to their mountain den. Lucius ends up being carried off as an ass by real robbers attacking the house. This may be seen as a form of punishment for his earlier refusal to accept the protection and favor of the Hypatans and their god of Laughter. Lucius may have been acquitted in the earlier 'trial,' but he is punished nevertheless in a manner he could never have imagined even in his 'accused' scenario. This scenario does in a sense come true: Lucius is 'condemned' to loss of life as a human and to exile. In these adventures the ass ceases to be in control of his own affairs as he passes from one community to another, being sold to various cruel masters and suffering all manner of trials and tribulations.[97]

The presence of certain themes from the Laughter festival narrative in Lucius' subsequent adventures as an ass makes the latter mirror the former. First, in his asinine adventures everybody is privy to a joke except for him, just as was the case in his earlier ordeal. Secondly, Lucius is reduced to the status of a complete outsider, just as he was a foreigner in Hypata. Finally, Lucius is reduced to his animal state by the same kind of misguided overconfidence he displayed towards magic before his painful experience in the Laughter festival. Hence Lucius' adventures as an ass may be said to replicate the ridicule he suffers in the theater.

The narrative of the Laughter festival exhibits a pervasive theatrical structure. The drunken Lucius unwittingly devises two plots: one for the morning of the festival, and one for the evening before. The Hypatans take advantage of Lucius' imaginings and put him on mock trial, which seems to acquire the function of a *dokimasia*, i.e. initiatory role-playing for communal integration. In the re-enactment of this ritual, all the participants act out roles: Lucius unwittingly plays both roles as criminal and as defendant in

---

[97] Bradley 2000, 110-25, treats Lucius' animalization as well as his ensuing hardships as a metaphor for the conditions slaves found themselves in Roman society.

order to prove the heroic nature of his deed. These two roles correspond to the two distinct plots acted out on the morning of the festival and on the night before it; the wineskins appear as robbers, the magistrates perform as *iudices*; the two women play the widows and mothers of the 'dead men,' and so forth. The town-magistrates offer Lucius exceptional honors for his brilliant performance in the Laughter festival. Such an offer is far removed from the notion of the protagonist as a scapegoat figure, as most critics take him to be. After all, Lucius has committed a triple 'murder,' for which he must undergo a ritual 'catharsis' before he can be integrated into the Hypatan community and their 'fellowship of Laughter.' Following the trial, Lucius is admitted into the Hypatan community with the new social status of 'honorary citizen.' He not only refuses the offer of integration, but continues to display the same naive overconfidence towards magic as before. This insistence leads to his transformation into an ass. The ensuing adventures appear to evoke themes that have originally appeared in the ordeal at the Laughter festival. The narrative of Lucius' asinine wanderings can therefore be viewed as a reflection of his misadventures in the town of Hypata.

Chapter II

Fatally Successful Performances

This chapter concentrates on cases of fatally successful performances in the lengthy narrative sequence known as the Charite-complex (4.22-8.14). In this part of the novel the emphasis is on disguise and trickery. These notions can best be seen in two sequences: (1) Tlepolemus' rescue of his bride Charite (7.1-14), and (2) the servant's tale of Charite's death (8.1-14). The first sequence reveals the fate awaiting the avaricious (the robbers), while the second constitutes a moral warning to those who are lustful (Thrasyllus). In both cases all major characters (i.e. Tlepolemus, Thrasyllus, and Charite) assume roles and succeed in their performances, but eventually meet a tragic death. Furthermore, the sequences are thematically interconnected: Tlepolemus presents himself as a friend to the robbers in order to liberate Charite from captivity in the robbers' cave, destroy the gang for their greed and then marry his bride. Similarly, Charite will later present herself as friend and potential wife to Thrasyllus in order to punish him for killing her husband and harboring sexual designs upon her. Having accomplished her plan, Charite is free to reunite with her husband in death, just as Tlepolemus had previously wedded her after successfully implementing his plan against the robbers. Her suicide is to some extent predictable, since it offers the only way to bring about a reunion with her husband in death. Moreover, Charite's scheme of revenge on Thrasyllus, her ensuing suicide, and Thrasyllus' death over the couple's grave are enhanced by imagery that alludes to Roman wedding rites. Nevertheless, all these 'marriages' end in disaster, revealing the absence of matrimonial bliss in the world of Lucius' asinine adventures.

1. The New Recruit's Tale of Plotina

In 7.1-13 the young Tlepolemus arrives at the robbers' cave disguised as Haemus the brigand, in order to take command, liberate Charite from captivity and destroy the gang who kidnapped her on her wedding night. Tlepolemus' plan is modeled on his own fictional tale of Plotina, which he narrates to the robbers as part of his overall scheme. Like Plotina, who dresses herself as a man and follows her husband into exile, Tlepolemus appears in disguise. Just as Caesar pardons the exiled husband as a reward and then orders the destruction of Haemus' gang, so Tlepolemus regains his bride and then returns to the lair to kill his former would-be followers and take their treasure. This reading presupposes an association between Tlepolemus/Haemus and Caesar, and not just between Tlepolemus and Plotina, as has been the prevailing view up to now. Thus the new recruit's tale of Plotina becomes a brilliant metaphor for the narrative containing it. The robbers fail to observe any resonance between the inner tale and its framing narrative and accept the new recruit in their band as their leader. As a result they meet the same ill-fated end as Haemus' gang in the tale of Plotina.

The similarities between the inner tale and its frame acquire an added dimension as Lucius adopts an actorial mode when recounting the story; he withholds certain pieces of information that must be in his possession when the narrative is delivered. Only towards the end of the sequence does the ass overhear a private conversation between the new recruit and the girl. He then identifies Haemus as Tlepolemus, thus elevating himself to the status of authoritative narrator.

Whereas other scholars have pointed out individual connections either between Plotina and Tlepolemus,[98] or between Plotina and Charite,[99] I concentrate on the mirroring of Plotina's actions in those of Tlepolemus in disguise. The assumption of different roles is conditioned by the frustrated groom's object/goal to liberate his bride from captivity, destroy the robber's band and then resume the wedding ceremony disrupted by the abduction.

In 7.1-2 a robber spy returns to the cave and informs his companions of the Hypatans' investigations regarding the theft of Milo's treasure. In his report, the scout advises the robbers not to worry, because the Hypatans have laid the blame with a certain Lucius for (a) entering Milo's house with false credentials, (b) seducing Milo's servant Fotis, (c) discovering the hiding place of Milo's treasure and (d) carrying it off.[100] Furthermore, according to the spy's report Lucius managed to outdistance his pursuers by fleeing the town on his horse. This information is misleading, because the Hypatans are not only mistaken about Lucius but also unaware of his metamorphosis into an ass. The same applies to the robbers, who bring Lucius and other pack animals to their cave entirely unawares.

---

[98] Hijmans Jr. *et al.* 1981, 3-4 and 123 (s.v. *zonis*).

[99] Tatum 1969, 518; Walsh 1970, 161. An exception is Tatum 1969, 506-07, who interprets the tale as a parody of the values set forth in the robber-tales of Book 4.

[100] For connections between Tlepolemus' disguise and that of Thrasyleon/bear, see Frangoulidis 1994, 337-348, and additional bibliography there.

In his capacity as narrator Lucius then hands himself over to his former self as an ass, who wishes to interrupt the spy and refute the accusations leveled by the Hypatans, but fails on account of his inability to speak. Structurally speaking, this loss of speech contrasts with his earlier brilliant role as orator in the performance at the Laughter festival, in which he was desperate to prove his innocence (see Ch. 1.3 above). The ass then sorrowfully recalls the cruel decision of the robbers to sew the girl into his belly and throw them both off a cliff. Thus Lucius' metamorphosis into an animal and his ensuing removal from Milo's house by the robbers reveal a lack of control over his own affairs.

When the spy learns that the gang's former leaders have been killed, he advises the robbers to draft further members (7.4). He has already done his duty in persuading a young man to abandon his life as beggar and join their ranks. In an ironic twist this new recruit turns out to be Tlepolemus. Thus the very same man who advises his companions not to worry becomes responsible for their death. The robbers agree to the spy's proposal and encourage him to bring in the newcomer, who in true beggar fashion is dressed in rags. As narrator the ass recounts the new recruit's self-introduction to the bandits (7.5):[101]

> 'havete,' inquit, 'fortissimo deo Marti clientes mihique iam fidi commilitones, et virum magnanimae vivacitatis volentem volentes accipite, libentius vulnera corpore excipientem quam aurum manu suscipientem ipsaque morte, quam formidant alii, meliorem. nec me putetis egenum vel abiectum neve de pannulis istis virtutes meas aestimetis. nam praefui validissimae manui totamque prorsus devastavi

---

[101] See above n. 3.

Macedoniam. ego sum praedo famosus Haemus ille
Thracius, cuius totae provinciae nomen horrescunt, patre
Therone aeque latrone inclito progntaus, humano sanguine
nutritus interque ipsos manipulos factionis educatus heres at
aemulus virtutis paternae.'

'Hail, brave servants of Mars and now my trusty fellow-
soldiers! Receive a willing recruit willingly. You see before
you a man of heroic vigour, who more gladly accepts wounds
on his body than gold in his hand, and who is superior to
death itself, which others fear. And do not think me destitute
or an outcast; do not judge my virtues from these rags. I was
in command of a strong and mighty band and laid waste the
whole of Macedonia. I am the famous brigand, Haemus the
Thracian, at whose name every province trembles. My father
was Theron, also a renowned robber; I was nursed on
human blood and raised among the squadrons of our troop
as heir and rival to my father's valour.'

Here Tlepolemus identifies himself as Haemus, the famous Thracian brigand. In etymological terms his name is related both to a mountain range in Thrace and to the Greek term *haima* (blood),[102] symbolizing the new blood which the robbers need, having lost all their leaders in earlier expeditions against towns in Boiotia (Book 4). The new recruit then proceeds to relate his fictional tale of the virtuous wife Plotina to the robbers (7.6-8).

In the tale certain jealous people make false accusations against Plotina's husband and succeed in having him exiled.[103] The virtuous Plotina then dresses herself as a man and follows her husband abroad. One night Haemus and his gang plan a night-raid

---

[102] Tatum 1969, 507; see also Kenney 1998, 243.
[103] Jealousy as a motive is common to both the new recruit's tale and the servant's later story of Charite's death.

on an inn where the exiled couple are staying. Plotina herself raises the alarm and forces the robbers to flee with a very limited haul. The wife then appeals to Caesar to recall her husband from exile. As a reward for her exceptional services in preventing the ransacking of the inn, Caesar grants her wish and orders the destruction of Haemus' band.

With regard to the actantial structure, Plotina's actions acquire the function of a plan in which the distribution of actors/characters may be arranged as follows: Plotina fills the position of the subject, her goal being to win her husband's recall from exile; the ill-favor of those who had Plotina's husband exiled out of jealousy appear as opponents; Caesar and his soldiers are helpers. Haemus and his gang seemingly appear in the position of the opponent. With the benefit of hindsight, however, they actually fill the helper's position as they assist Plotina to win her husband's recall. Finally, the exiled husband takes the receiver's place.

As internal narrator, Tlepolemus does not disclose his actual identity. Nevertheless, readers may begin to suspect that things are not as they seem, given the inordinately high praise Haemus heaps on his arch enemy Plotina. In retrospect, this amounts to little more than self-praise, since Tlepolemus is clearly presented as her substitute.

The new recruit's tale admirably reproduces the events of its framing narrative in almost every perspective. Firstly, Plotina's decision to dress herself as man and follow her husband into exile (7.6) recalls the plan devised by Tlepolemus to rescue his bride, one noticeable difference being that his disguise does not involve a reversal of gender (7.5). Secondly, the attempted ransacking of the inn by Haemus and his gang (7.7) resembles the robbers' assault on

Charite's home (4.22-27). Finally, Caesar's decision to grant Plotina's husband a pardon and order that Haemus and his gang be put to the sword (7.7) foreshadows the implementation of Telpolemus' plan, which involves him assuming command of the robbers. Once Charite has been brought home, Tlepolemus returns to the cave with a multitude of armed companions and pack animals, removes the treasure and kills all the robbers (7.9-12).[104] The similarities between Tlepolemus' tale of Plotina and the framing narrative make the latter a clear *mise en abyme*, or paradigm, for the former.

The newcomer then offers the robbers the money he has stolen from various houses (7.8), thus mimicking the scout's earlier offer of one thousand gold coins stolen from various travelers (7.4). The connection is strengthened by the detail that the scout offers the money to the robbers *after* delivering his false report, just as the new recruit offers coins *after* telling his fabricated tale of Plotina. When Tlepolemus seeks to assume leadership of the gang his proposal is accepted unanimously. The elegant robe offered to him as leader must be interpreted as a 'costume' for this new role; it accompanies the offer of a place of honor at the ensuing feast. As chief Haemus/Tlepolemus is in a position to implement his scheme and thus liberate his bride.

---

[104] In the Plotina tale, Haemus passes undetected through Caesar's soldiers by dressing himself as a woman. In the same guise he continues his life as a thief, holding for himself a bag of *viaticulum* stolen in attacks on towns along the way (7.8). This evokes Plotina, who dresses herself as a man, hides her gold and jewels in her girdle and follows her husband into exile (7.6). This thematic parallel, however, bears out a similarity between two people, Haemus and Plotina in the Plotina tale, rather than between one character in the tale, e.g. Plotina, and another in the frame narrative, e.g. Tlepolemus.

In the actantial structure, the distribution of actors/characters may appear as follows: Tlepolemus is the subject whose goal is to free his bride and destroy the robbers' gang. Charite appears in the position of the receiver; the robbers fill the opponent's place. The main helpers in Tlepolemus' disguise are his bride, perhaps the Plotina narrative (as it serves to win over the robbers' confidence) and above all Tlepolemus' wine, which puts the robbers to sleep and enables the escape from the cave. The ass can also be considered as helper after he has fully comprehended the situation.

Tlepolemus then puts his scheme into action. He finds out about the robbers' plan to kill the girl together with the ass and proposes instead to sell her to a pimp (7.9):

> 'non sum quidem tam brutus vel certe temerarius' inquit 'ut scitum vestrum inhibeam, sed malae conscientiae reatum intra me sustinebo, si quod bonum mihi videtur dissimulavero. sed prius fiduciam vestri causa sollicito mihi tribuite, cum praesertim vobis, si sententia haec mea displicuerit, liceat rursus ad asinum redire. nam ego arbitror latrones, quique eorum recte sapiunt, nihil anteferre lucro suo debere ac ne ipsam quidem saepe et aliis damnosam ultionem. ergo igitur si perdideritis in asino virginem, nihil amplius quam sine ullo compendio indignationem vestram exercueritis. quin ego censeo deducendam eam ad quampiam civitatem ibique venundandam. nec enim levi pretio distrahi poterit talis aetatula. nam et ipse quosdam lenones pridem cognitos habeo, quorum poterit unus magnis equidem talentis, ut arbitror, puellam istam praestinare condigne natalibus suis fornicem processuram nec in similem fugam discursuram, non nihil etiam, cum lupanari servierit, vindictae vobis depensuram. hanc ex animo quidem meo sententiam conducibilem protuli; sed vos vestrorum estis consiliorum rerumque domini.'

'I am not so stupid,' he said, 'nor certainly so rash as to try to repress your ordinance. But I will suffer internally from the guilt of a bad conscience if I conceal my considered opinion. First of all, put your confidence in me: it is on your account that I am concerned. And at any rate if you do not approve my proposal you can always return to the ass. Now I believe that bandits, those at least who think straight, should put nothing ahead of their own profit, not even revenge, which often recoils upon the avenger. Therefore, if you destroy the maiden in the ass, you will have accomplished nothing other than exercising your resentment at no gain. My recommendation is rather that she should be taken off to some city and sold there. A girl of her tender age can be retailed at no small price. I myself have some old friends who are pimps, and I am sure one of them will be able to purchase your girl for big money, as befits her background. She will go into a brothel, and will not run away and escape again; furthermore, by her enslavement to a whorehouse she will be paying off your revenge. I have laid this advantageous proposal before you in all sincerity, but you yourselves are the masters of your own decisions and property.'

In this passage, Tlepolemus' proposal is fully in accord with the verisimilitude of events: in 4.23 the ass as narrator described the girl as exceptionally beautiful: *puellam mehercules et asino tali concupiscendam*. There are two alternative solutions with regard to the destiny of a captive girl portrayed as exceptionally beautiful: either to 'buy' her freedom and then marry her or sell her to a *leno* for profit. Haemus has little difficulty in arguing for the more profitable second alternative. This solution suits the robbers, who had originally kidnapped the girl in order to obtain a high ransom from her rich parents.¹⁰⁵ After a long deliberation, they agree to the new recruit's proposal and remove her chains: *protinus vinculis exsolvunt virginem* (7.10). As narrator, the ass characterizes the new recruit as *sospitator egregius*, excellent savior of both the girl and himself, because the new proposal averts the robbers' cruel plan to put the girl in his belly and then throw them both off a cliff.

On seeing the new recruit and hearing his reference to the brothel and the pimp, the girl bursts into joyful laughter: *coepit risu laetissimo gestire* (7.10). Her reaction implies recognition of her groom (and consequently of his plot), but the ass foolishly interprets her laughter as signaling her delight at the prospect of becoming a prostitute. As a result he is led to reflect on the debase nature of all women. In their differing responses, the girl and the ass occupy two distinct positions in the actantial structure: the former acts as Tlepolemus' helper, whereas the latter unwittingly plays the opponent, mainly because of his total inability to comprehend the world around him.¹⁰⁶

In his role as Haemus Tlepolemus goes on to propose that the robbers make a sacrifice to their deity, Mars, and then sell the girl in order to draft new members into the gang with the profits obtained. Since there is no wine in the cave, Tlepolemus takes ten of his companions to storm a nearby *castellum* to obtain cattle and

---

¹⁰⁵ Winkler 1985, 48. Tlepolemus' liberation of his bride from captivity contains a web of allusions to the marital rites; on this see Frangoulidis 1996, 196-202. For discussion of allusions to the wedding ritual in the scene of Charite's abduction by the robbers in 4.26-28, see Papaioannou 1998, 307-312.

¹⁰⁶ Winkler 1985, 47, interprets the differing responses of the ass and the girl to the new recruit's proposal as a brilliant case of first-time and second-time readings.

wine for their forthcoming dinner.[107] He soon returns to the cave, sacrifices a large billy-goat to Mars and lays on the feast. In preparing the food he assumes the role previously occupied by the old nurse, who hanged herself in 6.30 because she was unable to prevent an earlier attempted escape by the ass and the girl.

During the robbers' banquet Tlepolemus often visits his bride in her cell, offering her food and wine on the pretext of fetching items for the dinner, thus reverting to his role as the girl's groom. As narrator, the ass unknowingly criticizes the girl for forgetting her groom, eagerly accepting food from the brigand and passionately responding to his kisses (7.11):

> 'hem oblita es nuptiarum tuique mutui cupitoris, puella virgo, et illi nescio cui recenti marito, quem tibi parentes iunxerunt, hunc advenam cruentumque percussorem praeponis? nec te conscientia stimulat, sed adfectione calcata inter lanceas et gladios istos scortari tibi libet? quid, si quo modo latrones ceteri persenserint? non rursum recurres ad asinum et rursum exitium mihi parabis? re vera ludis de alieno corio.'

> 'What! Have you forgotten your wedding and the man who shares your desires, young lady? Do you prefer this stranger, this bloody assassin, to that new husband of yours, whoever he is, to whom your parents wed you? Doesn't your conscience prick you? Or do you like to trample on affections and play the whore amid these spears and swords? What if the other robbers somehow find out? Will you not go right back to the ass again? And procure my destruction again? Truly you are playing games with someone else's hide.'

In this soliloquy, the ass foolishly thinks that the girl prefers the assassin to her groom, thereby putting his own life at risk; for if the robbers were to discover all, they would revert to their original

---

[107] Tlepolemus' ten companions evoke Plotina as mother of ten children.

plan. In wrongly accusing the girl, Lucius the ass appears in the same position as the Hypatans, who previously mistakenly accused him of robbing his host.[108] An intratextual reading at this point reveals a telling contrast between Psyche and Charite. The former exposes her husband's concealed identity, marking the beginning of her wanderings in search of the man who abandoned her, whereas the latter does not disclose Tlepolemus' disguise and eventually reunites with him.

Soon, however, the ass overhears a private conversation between the girl and the thief in which Tlepolemus discloses the girl's name: *'bono animo es,' inquit, 'Charite dulcissima; nam totos istos hostes tuos statim captivos habebis'* (7.12).[109] The girl's name had remained concealed since her first entrance in the narrative (Book 4)[110] and, in revealing it, Tlepolemus simultaneously sheds his own 'mask' as Haemus the brigand. At this point the ass characterizes himself as a sycophant and re-identifies the new recruit as Tlepolemus, the girl's young groom. This signals his full grasp of the Haemus narrative and brings him into sharp contrast with the robbers, whose failure to read between the lines leads to an ill-fated end. At the same time the new-found knowledge triggers a switch in the ass' position in the actantial structure, from unwitting opponent to Tlepolemus' plan to that of his helper. Tlepolemus remains cautious, continually offering wine to the robbers until he

---

[108] Shumate 1999, 122.

[109] Sandy 1999, 93, observes that the withholding of Tlepolemus' name by the narrator allows Apuleius to exploit the hypothesis of the novel that the narrator-ass has retained his mental faculties.

[110] For the conditions under which Charite's name is revealed, see Frangoulidis 1991 (b), 387-394.

gets them all drunk. Once they are all comatose he binds them in fetters, thus fulfilling his earlier promise to the girl to change her captors into her captives (7.12).[111]

Tlepolemus then puts his bride on the ass and safely exits the cave. The liberation of Charite and the ass from captivity finds a distant analogy in Caesar's recall of the husband from exile in the earlier fabricated tale of Plotina (7.7). As narrator, the ass describes the spectacle of Tlepolemus' homecoming and Charite riding on the ass with the military imagery of a triumphant return: *memorandum spectamen, virginem asino triumphantem* (7.13). The presence of such imagery is justifiable, since in liberating his bride Tlepolemus/Haemus has earlier assumed a role analogous to that of Caesar when he granted a pardon to Plotina's husband.

Having entrusted Charite to her parents, Telpolemus returns to the cave with a multitude of armed companions, the ass and other pack animals. Some of the robbers are put to the sword and others are thrown off a cliff, thus establishing an analogy with Caesar's soldiers when they kill all of Haemus' companions (7.7). In both cases the robbers are punished for their crimes and avarice. The booty stored in the cave is loaded onto the animals, brought back to town and turned over to public custody. After Tlepolemus' homecoming Charite's parents formally marry their daughter to him, thus concluding the ceremony so brutally disrupted by the abduction.

---

[111] For the Odyssean elements in the scene see Frangoulidis 1992 (a); also Harrison 1990, 198-200, who interprets Tlepolemus' plot as echoing the stratagem of the disguised Odysseus among the suitors.

As we have seen, the narrative of Tlepolemus' rescue of his bride and the ass from captivity evokes themes that first appear in his own fabricated tale of the virtuous wife Plotina. In failing to notice any resemblance between 'fiction' and 'reality,' the robbers condemn themselves to the fate of Haemus' gang. These similarities gain an added dimension as a result of the withholding of known information. The actorial narrative strategy helps create suspense and reinforces the theatricality of Tlepolemus' disguise. Only towards the end of his narrative does the ass recount a private conversation he overheard between the new recruit and Charite. At this point, the ass finally realizes that Haemus the brigand is no more than a clever disguise. Armed with this discovery Lucius the ass acquires full authoritative command of his narrative.

2. A Faithful Wife's Revenge:
The Servant's Tale of Charite

Book 8 opens with the arrival of Charite's servant, who announces the tragic death of his mistress to his assembled colleagues and relates the destruction of the entire household (8.1-14). The tragic tone of the tale is understandable, given that the narrator is personally affected by the events he speaks of.

In the tale, a rejected former suitor named Thrasyllus devises a scheme to gain Charite's hand in marriage by killing Tlepolemus during a hunt. After the ghost of Tlepolemus has appeared in a dream and revealed the true circumstances surrounding his death, his widow concocts a scheme to take revenge on the lustful and wily Thrasyllus. The anti-hero's cunning in killing Tlepolemus is mirrored in similarities between Charite's revenge scheme and the boar-hunt plot, while his sexual ambitions are mocked in a plan which exploits aspects of the wedding ritual.

To be persuasive, the (fictional) marriage ritual, like the hunting scheme before it, requires role playing and gender role-reversal, so that the heroine may punish her opponent most appropriately for his iniquity. The wedding imagery is further reinforced at the conclusion of the tale: Charite's suicide on her husband's tomb is represented as a (re)marriage in death, as it re-enacts aspects of the wedding ritual following Tlepolemus' liberation of his bride from the robbers. In the end, Thrasyllus' suicide by starvation is also represented as a marriage in death, as suggested in Charite's angry monologue before she attacks her enemy in his sleep.

Our object here is to demonstrate Thrasyllus' change of roles and how they in turn determine the roles adopted by Charite in the application of her revenge scheme. Wedding imagery enhances the scheme and serves to intensify the tragedy of the narrative. As we have said, all three marriages in this section of the novel end in disaster, despite the (apparent) success of their respective schemes.[112] This irony underlines the impossibility of conjugal bliss in the world of Lucius' asinine adventures.

---

[112] This tale has been discussed extensively in relation to its literary reminiscences. For Apuleius' borrowings from Vergil see the discussion in Forbes 1943, 39-40, and Finkelpearl 1986, 139-61. See also Hijmans Jr. *et al.* 1985, *ad loc.*; Frangoulidis 1992 (b), 435-50; Shumate 1996 (b), 103-16; and recently, Harrison 1997, 63-65. Westerbrink 1978, 70, offers a list of parallels between the episode of Tlepolemus' death, and the Adrastus story in Herodotus' *Histories* (1.34-45); also recently Repath 2000, 628. Finally, Griffiths 1978, 151-2, associates the incident of the boar-hunt with the myth of Adonis.

The servant begins his tale with a brief character sketch, in which he describes the chequered career of Thrasyllus. The fact that he is portrayed as having fallen into the company of thieves brings to mind those involved in the earlier abduction: *factionibus latronum male sociatus nec non etiam manus infectus humano cruore* (8.1). Among other things the narrator relates Thrasyllus' unsuccessful attempts at wooing Charite when she reached marriageable age. Several of the facts must have been familiar to the slaves who constitute the audience of the servant's tale, but the narrator retells them so that they, and by extension we, may have a comprehensive view of the action. We learn that Thrasyllus was originally rejected as a suitor on account of his lax *mores: morum tamen inprobatus* (8.2). The biographical passage thus acquires a functional significance in the narrative.

Following Charite's liberation and her subsequent marriage to Tlepolemus, Thrasyllus conceals his criminal intentions, plays the role of the couple's trusted friend and hence gains admission into their house: *occultato consilio sceleris, amici fidelissimi personam mentiebatur* (8.2). His physical proximity to Charite fires his lust for her. There is a contrast between *Cupido*, who provokes Thrasyllus' lust for Charite, and the conjugal love Tlepolemus inspires in his widow, as illustrated when the heroine posthumously represents him as Liber/Dionysus. The former destroys Charite's happy marriage to Tlepolemus, while the latter reunites the separated couple, albeit in death. In intratextual terms, Cupid as destroyer of marriages recalls the old woman's reference to him in 4.30 as: *omnium matrimonia corrumpens*. Thrasyllus quite literally becomes a thief of Charite's happy marriage to Tlepolemus, as Charite identifies him in 8.13: *funestum mearum nuptiarum praedonem*.

Thrasyllus devises his scheme the moment he realizes he is unable to approach Charite on account of the guards around her.

The narrator makes an apostrophe to his audience as he is about to narrate Thrasyllus' trickery in the hunt (8.3):

> spectate denique, sed, oro, sollicitis animis intendite, quorsum furiosae libidinis proruperint impetus.
>
> So watch—and please pay careful attention and you will see the result of the violent attacks of insane passion.

In this address, the use of the imperative *spectate* has a theatre-specific meaning which draws attention to the theatrical aspect of Thrasyllus' scheme. In this way the narrator can help both the internal and the external audience to visualize the events of his tale.

One day Tlepolemus goes on a hunt for wild goats, taking Thrasyllus with him. In the actantial model, the actors/characters may occupy the following positions: Tlepolemus and Thrasyllus appear in the place of the subject; the goal/object is to hunt. In this model Tlepolemus also occupies the position of the sender; both Tlepolemus and Thrasyllus fill the receiver position; the horses along with the various instruments of the hunt serve as helpers.

In spatial terms the hunt marks a shift from the interior of Charite's home to the wide open spaces. Charite expressly forbids her husband to hunt wild animals other than deer and wild goats (8.4). Her instructions reveal a concern for Telpolemus' safety while suggesting a feminine side to his identity that contrasts starkly with the cunning he displayed at the robbers' den (Ch. II.1).

During the hunt a savage boar appears, prompting the terrified servants to dash for cover behind foliage and trees. From this ideal location, the narrator in his role as participant can watch events unfold, thereby substantiating the eyewitness account of his narrative.

On seeing the boar Thrasyllus finds a brilliant chance to put his devious scheme into action. Through a clever appeal to manhood he urges Tlepolemus to pursue the boar, in direct contravention of Charite's order not to hunt wild beasts armed with tusk and horn (8.5):

> '[q]uid stupore confusi vel etiam cassa formidine similes humilitati servorum istorum vel in modum pavoris feminei deiecti tam opimam praedam mediis manibus amittimus? quin equos inscendimus? quin ocius indipiscimur? en cape uenabulum et ego sumo lanceam.'
>
> 'Why are we standing here confused and dumbfounded, needlessly afraid like our lowborn slaves there, or cowed like frightened women? Why are we letting such a rich prize slip through our hands? Why not mount our horses and quickly catch up with him? You take a hunting spear, and I will get a lance.'

When the quarry is at close quarters Tlepolemus throws his lance, leaving himself unarmed. At the very same moment Thrasyllus throws a javelin at the thigh of his companion's horse, causing it to fall to the ground: *supinatus invitus dominum suum devolvit ad terram* (8.5). This point marks a transition from the previous actantial structure to another, corresponding to the plot devised by Thrasyllus. From his role as hunter Telpolemus becomes the quarry in place of the boar—subject and object exchange positions. Thrasyllus is helper until he pierces Tlepolemus in the thigh and then kills the boar with ease, at which point he becomes subject. The boar's tusks and the hunting weapons are to be seen as helpers throughout.

Thrasyllus is confident that the wound in Tlepolemus' thigh will appear to have been inflicted by the boar's tusks: *per femus dexterum dimisit lanceam tanto ille quidem fidentius, quanto crederet ferri vulnera similia futura prosectu dentium* (8.5). This wound is designed to prevent Tlepolemus from running away and saving himself from the savage beast. That being said, Thrasyllus is the actual murderer. As Dowden points out, the boar is not boarish enough and so Thrasyllus takes over, substituting himself for the animal and then killing it: *nec non tamen ipsam quoque bestiam facili manu transadigit* (8.5).[113]

There are two features in the narrative which help to strengthen the association between Thrasyllus and the beast, thus making their substitution valid:[114] first, the fiery look of the boar recalls Thrasyllus' passion for Charite, represented in the narrative by fire imagery (*oculis aspectu minaci flammeus, impetu saevo frementis oris totus fulmineus* 8.4 ~ *furiosae libidinis proruperint impetus* 8.3); and second, the boar's tusks can be compared with Thrasyllus' javelin, so much so that both are said to leave the same marks on flesh.

In the context of the planned marriage to Charite, Tlepolemus' death may be interpreted as a prenuptial sacrifice, thus mirroring his earlier offering of various animals at temples and public places prior to the wedding: *ad nuptias ... templis et aedibus*

---

[113] Dowden 1993, 104.

[114] The implicit presence of wedding imagery in the servant's tragic tale of Charite has received little scholarly attention. Barrett 1994, 60-74, has devoted a detailed discussion to the marriages of Psyche and Charite, but he examines them in relation to their importance for the development of Lucius as a character in the novel.

publicis victimas immolabat (4.26).[115] Not long afterwards Tlepolemus arrives at the robbers' den disguised as Haemus the brigand, liberates his bride and completes the previously interrupted wedding ceremony. Thus the two disruptions of the marriage, occurring as they do at either end of the Charite-complex, emphasize the futility of efforts to separate the beloved couple both in life and in death.

The narrator mocks the illusion of Thrasyllus' role as he embraces Tlepolemus and mourns him, allegedly in great sorrow (8.6). At this point his behavior is reminiscent of the widow in the Thelyphron tale, and lies in stark contrast to the genuine grief experienced by Charite. Later on in the funeral, Thrasyllus calls his rival 'dear friend,' 'companion' and even 'brother' (8.7), deceiving even the goddess *Veritas* herself. Once near Charite, however, Thrasyllus attempts to touch her, thus making his actual intentions clear. His proximity to Charite after the boar-hunt contrasts with his inability to approach her when her husband was alive (8.3), and, in retrospect, accounts for his murderous scheme.

After Telpolemus is laid to rest, grief-stricken Charite sets her mind on committing suicide by starvation. Thrasyllus tries to prevent her death-plan by appealing to her parents, who intervene at the last moment. Nevertheless, Charite is unable to overcome the loss of her husband; she has his image made in the likeness of

---

[115] For the sacrifice before the *deductio*, see Treggiari 1991, 164, who further observes that the groom usually does not attend the *deductio*. She cautions, however, that the details of the groom's role in this procedure are sketchy. For a discussion of aspects of the wedding ritual in the episode of Charite's abduction by the thieves (4.26-28), see Papaioannou 1998, 307-312.

Liber/Dionysus, and worships him as a god (8.7).[116] This is appropriate, given that Tlepolemus used the Dionysian weapon to overcome the robbers. Hunting is yet another activity associated with Dionysus. Such imagery in the tale helps to characterize Charite as a 'maenad' and, in turn, foreshadows the tragic fate that awaits Thrasyllus, her opponent and victim.

Although Charite is still mourning, Thrasyllus renews his sexual hold on her by proposing marriage, thus living up to the etymology of his name, which derives from the Greek noun *thrasus*, 'bold,' and the diminutive suffix -yllus.[117] Charite declines the proposal with animal howls: *ferinos mugitus iterans* (8.8),[118] a reaction entirely consistent with her portrayal as a bacchant in 8.6, when Fama brought her news of Tlepolemus' death: *amens et vecordia percita cursuque bacchata furibundo ... insana voce casum mariti quiritans*. Moreover, she begins to suspect that Thrasyllus has had a hand in her husband's death: *et iam scaenam pessimi Thrasylli perspiciens* (8.8). In the event she manages to calm down and asks the suitor to give her some time, ostensibly so as to consider his proposal, but in reality so as to plan her revenge. In the meantime, the ghost of Tlepolemus appears to Charite in a dream and describes the circumstances of his death (8.8):

---

[116] Hijmans Jr. 1986, 355-56 develops the association of Tlepolemus with Liber/Dionysus throughout the Charite-complex on the basis of several traits that Tlepolemus shares with the god. Dowden 1993, 101, sees a contrast between Tlepolemus' apotheosis as Liber and Thrasyllus' bestialization.

[117] On this etymology see Barrett 1994, 79. On the other hand, Repath 2000, 627-300, discerns an association between Thrasyllus, the Platonist/Pythagorean philosopher, and an Adrastus, the Peripatetic, given that in Apuleius' tale Thrasyllus plays the Adrastus-figure.

[118] For a discussion of the animal imagery in the tale, see Shumate 1996 (b), 106.

'[m]i coniux, quod tibi prorsus ab alio dici non licebit: etsi pectori tuo iam permarcet nostri memoria vel acerbae mortis meae casus foedus caritatis intercidit,—quovis alio felicius maritare, modo ne in Thrasylli manum sacrilegam convenias neve sermonem conferas nec mensam accumbas nec toro adquiescas. fuge mei percussoris cruentam dexteram. noli parricidio nuptias auspicari. vulnera illa, quorum sanguinem tuae lacrimae proluerunt, non sunt tota dentium vulnera: lancea mali Thrasylli me tibi fecit alienum.'

'My wife,' he began 'for no one else can ever call you by that name: even though the memory of me still abides [*permaneat*] in your heart, nevertheless the misfortune of my bitter death has cut through the bonds of love; marry someone else and be happy, only do not accept the impious hand of Thrasyllus. Do not speak with him, nor share his table, nor sleep in his bed. Flee the blood-stained hand of my killer. Do not enter into a marriage polluted by murder. Those wounds whose blood your tears washed away are not all the marks of tusks. It was the spear of evil Thrasyllus that separated me from you.'

The ghost provides Charite with information she was previously unaware of, not having participated in the hunt. Although he does not forbid his widow to remarry anyone else, he explicitly advises her to reject Thrasyllus, whom he identifies as his murderer. In structural terms, this instruction parallels Charite's earlier order not to hunt animals with tusks and horns (8.4).

After learning the true circumstances of her husband's death, Charite ceases behaving like a bacchant and instead assumes the role of a trickster figure. She resolves to take revenge on her opponent and then die, but does not divulge her plans to anyone. Consequently, she assumes the role of Thrasyllus' friend and turns down his marriage proposal with dignity when he resumes courting (8.9 *emphasis is mine*):

'*[a]dhuc,*' inquit, 'tui fratris meique carissimi mariti facies pulchra illa in meis deversatur oculis, *adhuc* odor cinnameus ambrosei corporis per nares meas percurrit, *adhuc* formonsus Tlepolemus in meo vivit pectore. boni ergo et optimi consules, si luctui legitimo miserrimae feminae necessarium concesseris tempus, quoad residuis mensibus spatium reliquum compleatur anni, quae res cum meum pudorem, tum etiam tuum salutare commodum respicit, ne forte inmaturitate nuptiarum indignatione iusta manes acerbos mariti ad exitium salutis tuae suscitemus.'

'The beautiful face of your brother and my husband,' she said, 'still dwells in my eyes; the cinnamon scent of his heavenly body still runs through my nostrils; handsome Tlepolemus still lives in my heart. You will be acting, therefore, in your own best interest if you allow a poor unhappy woman the legally required period of mourning, until the remaining months fill out the balance of a year's time. This is a matter not only of my honour, but also of your own safety and advantage, since with a premature marriage we might incite my husband's bitter ghost to rise up in just indignation and put an end to your life.'

In this passage Charite buys time by extolling her husband's beauty in death and by appealing to decorum. Thus she can sharpen her plan of revenge. The triple repetition of the adverb *adhuc* underlines Charite's devotion to the memory of Tlepolemus and stresses Thrasyllus' precipitation in proposing marriage so soon after the funeral.[119] Charite's decision to veil her hostile intentions mirrors Thrasyllus himself, who earlier had concealed his plan to kill his rival Tlepolemus by playing the friend of the happily

---

[119] The description of Tlepolemus, whose divine body is presented as emitting heavenly scents, contrasts with the earlier presentation of his widow neglecting herself while mourning: *incuria squalida* (8.7).

married couple (8.2). In 8.9, Charite tries to turn down the proposal of her suitor, identifying him as Tlepolemus' brother, *tui fratris*, although she is by now deeply aware of his role in her husband's death.

When Thrasyllus fails to come to his senses, Charite becomes even more determined to carry out her plan. She pretends to accept the marriage proposal and invites Thrasyllus to come to her home alone, around the first night watch, concealed in his cloak (8.10):

> 'sed heus tu,' inquit Charite, 'quam probe veste contectus omnique comite viduatus prima vigilia tacitus fores meas accedas unoque sibilo contentus nutricem istam meam opperiare, quae claustris adhaerens excubabit adventui tuo. nec setius patefactis aedibus acceptum te nullo lumine conscio ad meum perducet cubiculum.'

> 'But be sure now,' urged Charite, 'that you come well covered by your cloak, and alone without a single companion. At the first watch come to my door in silence, give just one whistle, and wait for my nurse. She will be close by the locked door watching for your arrival, and as soon as she lets you in she will bring you to my bedroom, with no lamp to give us away.'

The apparent goal/value of Charite's scheme is the forming of a clandestine marriage when, in fact, she intends to punish her opponent for his crimes and then commit suicide. The difference between apparent and actual objects creates tension in the narrative and highlights Charite's scheme. Thrasyllus fails to perceive the ambiguity apparent in Charite's double goal, as is clear from his delight on hearing her proposal: *[p]lacuit Thrasyllo scaena feralium nuptiarum* (8.11).

Commentators have interpreted Charite's scheme as *coitus*,[120] whereas it should properly be interpreted as clandestine marriage. In 8.12, Charite herself employs the technical term for marriage, *nuptiae*, when she speaks to Thrasyllus, who is buried in sleep and fantasizing about marrying her: *nuptias non frueris*. The fact that this union is to be kept secret until the necessary period of mourning passes increases its resonance with aspects of the wedding ritual.

There are several elements in Charite's scheme that help characterize it as a secret wedding. First, Charite instructs Thrasyllus to visit her covered in his cloak: *quam probe veste contectus* (8.10): the covering of Thrasyllus' head evokes a distant parallel with the veiling of the bride in the Roman ceremony.[121] The bridal veil is traditionally removed either during the banquet, which takes place in the bride's new home, or in the more private setting of the

---

[120] *Pace* Hijmans Jr. *et al.* 1985, 112 (s.v. *nuptiarum*). On the other hand, Drake 2000, 16, defines the scheme as a *rendez-vous*. Compare the difference between Charite's scheme and the arrival of the lover Philesitherus in Book 9, who comes to Arete's home for lovemaking at night while her husband Barbarus is away (9.20).

[121] In Catullus 61.6-10 the marriage-god, Hymen, is invoked to appear wearing flowers underneath the bridal veil, just like brides in Roman weddings:

> cinge tempora floribus
> suave olentis amaraci,
> flammeum cape laetus, huc
> huc veni, niveo gerens
> luteum pede soccum.

> wreathe your temples with the flowers
> of the sweet smelling marjoram,
> take up the bridal veil joyfully and come here,
> come here, wearing on your snow-white
> foot the yellow slipper.

> (tr. Godwin)

bedroom, in front of the groom.[122] Thrasyllus being presented here as a veiled female is balanced by the portrayal of Charite in 8.11, bursting into the room with 'manly courage,' *masculis animis*.[123] Second, Thrasyllus should come to Charite's home at around the first night-watch, *prima vigilia* (8.10), which coincides with the timing of the bridal *deductio*, which takes place at night.[124] Finally, Charite's trusted nurse, who will wait for Thrasyllus behind the door and supposedly lead him (*perducet*) to Charite's bed chamber (*cubiculum*), plays the ritual role of *pronuba* whose duty is to help the bride cross the threshold of her new home, and then perform the *dextrarum iunctio*, i.e. the union of the couple.[125] The term *perducere* is close to *ducere*, which is the technical term for taking a wife, *ducere uxorem*.

Thrasyllus comes to Charite's home unaccompanied at dead of night, dressed as instructed: *ex imperio Charites adornatus* (8.11). The revenge scheme takes place in the inner space of a house, in contrast to Thrasyllus' deceit, which took place in the open space of the wild. The house functions as an inner stage where the performance of the scheme is expected to take place. The nurse welcomes Thrasyllus and offers him several cups of wine, informing him that her mistress has been delayed because her

---

[122] See Rehm 1994, 142.

[123] Schlam 1992, 76, argues that Charite's transformation into a man is designed to demonstrate that courage is not an exclusively male quality. It also serves as a structural parallel to Tlepolemus' feminine role in the episode of the hunt, when he was forbidden by his wife to hunt dangerous beasts. In 8.5, Thrasyllus encourages Tlepolemus to abandon his hesitation to hunt wild animals, which he defines as fear, the characteristic of women: *pavoris feminei*.

[124] Rehm 1994, 14, points out that the bride is led to the groom's house at night, unlike the funeral procession, which takes place during daylight.

[125] Williams 1958, 21.

parents have fallen ill.[126] The use of wine helps to maintain the amatory atmosphere of the scene as well as evoke a version of a wedding feast. It coincides with the overall Dionysian imagery of the tale by alluding to Bacchus, god of wine. Thrasyllus, whose suspicions are not aroused by Charite's absence, foolishly drinks the intoxicating wine and falls asleep on his back: *iamque eo ad omnes iniurias exposito ac supinato* (8.11). His defenselessness recreates the setting of Tlepolemus' falling off his injured horse: *toto tergo supinatus invitus dominum suum devolvit ad terram* (8.5). The participle *supinato* (8.11) recalls the earlier occurrence of the term in the boar-hunt scheme, *supinatum* (8.5). Thus, the nurse in her role as *pronuba* turns the eminent hunter into prey and then calls in her mistress.

At this moment, Charite bursts into the room with manly courage and raging force (*masculis animis impetuque diro fremens* 8.11), in a posture that dispels the illusion of her scheme and reveals her actual goal. She then angrily addresses Thrasyllus, who has fallen asleep in a drunken stupor (8.12). In this speech, Charite sarcastically addresses her opponent as 'faithful friend' (*fidus ... comes*), 'excellent hunter' (*venator ... egregius*), and 'dear husband' (*carus maritus*), thus identifying Thrasyllus' three fictional roles within the tale's narrative: (a) Tlepolemus' trusted friend; (b) hunter of the boar; and (c) Charite's husband. Moreover, Charite states her intention to pluck out Thrasyllus' eyes before taking her own life.

---

[126] In the case of Pseudo-Lucian's *Onos*, Anderson 1976, 63, considers the account of Homer's Polyphemus as a model for Charite's blinding of Thrasyllus. Hijmans Jr. 1986, 360-61, has accepted Anderson's proposition in light of its interesting implications. For the Odyssean elements in the scene, see Frangoulidis 1992 (b), 444-45. For the association between Charite's blinding Thrasyllus and Tlepolemus' punishing his bride's abductors, see Hijmans Jr. *et al.* 1985, 115-16 (s.v. *sepelivit ad somnum*).

This form of punishment was rooted in the belief that blindness is worse than death (a kind of refreshing sleep) and contrasts here with the way Thrasyllus killed Tlepolemus using a sharp weapon. Blinding is a fitting retribution for the suitor's crimes, since his lustful eyes have been marked in the narrative as the cause of the tragic end to Charite's marriage: *oculi isti, quibus male placui* (8.12; also later: *vivo tibi morientur oculi* 8.12).[127] This punishment has a normalizing and exemplary effect, and therefore reinforces acceptable marital behavior in society.

Before administering the punishment Charite ponders whether her delay allows her arch enemy to dream of her caresses: *meos forsitan tibi pestiferos imaginaris amplexos?* (8.12). The reference to Thrasyllus' lustful fantasies highlights the illusory nature of his sexual expectations. Charite calls on her enemy to awake from his drunken stupor to the actual darkness that awaits him when she plucks out his eyes. The punishment is metaphorically represented as an alternative wedding ceremony, at which the avenging Furies will be Thrasyllus' bridesmaids in place of the nurse, and *orbitas*, deprivation, will serve as his bride in place of Charite. In performance terms, Charite here exposes to the sleeping Thrasyllus the illusion of his expectations. Charite then executes the physical

---

[127] The blinding of Thrasyllus can also be interpreted as castration for his immoral designs on her. James 1987, 206, n. 28, observes that castration was a legal way of punishing adulterers. She cites Devereux 1973, 40-1, who in his analysis of Sophocles' *Oedipus* hints at a possible association between blinding and castration. She observes, however, that "if the blinding of Thrasyllus can, in a way, be represented as a symbolic act of castration (in punishment for the contemplated adultery alone), it then becomes associated with the proposed gelding of Lucius for his excessive sexual appetite. The ass/hero is saved from castration. Thrasyllus is sacrificed in his place."

part of her revenge, plucking out Thrasyllus' eyes with her hairpin.[128]

The punishment may be read in various ways. First, it brings to a head the perverted use of wedding imagery in Charite's scheme, pointing to the consummation of the wedding rites. This reading becomes possible by the fact that the apparent goal/object of Charite's scheme is her clandestine marriage to Thrasyllus. In this context, the hairpin as a sharp instrument symbolizes the phallus;[129] the eyes function as a substitute for the female sexual organ; and the outpouring of blood from the wounds symbolizes the deflowering of the bride on her wedding night. The phallic symbolism of the hairpin accords well with the overall theme of gender role-reversal brought about during the re-enactment of the marital ritual itself. In this regard Charite's change of role makes her a substitute for her deceased husband, possessing the body of the 'familiar' avenger and exacting 'blood-justice' on the murderer.

Alternatively, the blinding of Thrasyllus may be interpreted as castration, an established literary motif for the punishment of adulterers. Several examples from Roman comedy confirm this view: (1) in Plautus' *Miles Gloriosus*, the old bachelor Periplectomenus threatens to castrate the soldier Pyrgopolynices for his sexual advances towards his supposed wife, the courtesan Acroteleution (1394-98); (2) in *Mercator*, the *senex* Demipho is

---

[128] James 1987, 197-98, develops an association between Charite putting out Thrasyllus' eyes and Psyche exposing the concealed identity of the sleeping Cupid.

[129] Although Adams 1982, 14, does not list the term *acus* in his discussion, he observes that "[n]o objects are more readily likened to the penis than sharp instruments."

afraid that his wife will castrate him for his planned involvement in an extramarital affair with the *meretrix* Pasicompsa: *metu ne uxor me castret mea* (274); and (3) in Terence's *Eunuchus*, the young Chaerea is threatened with castration for raping the girl Pamphila, the foster sister of Thais, since the girl is an Athenian citizen: *nunc minatur porro sese id quod moechis solet* (957). Moreover, in the context of Charite's plan to punish her opponent's lustfulness, the sharp hairpin may symbolically be interpreted as phallus and the eyes may acquire the symbolic meaning of testicles. In intratextual terms this is yet another example of emasculation as punishment, a theme familiar to us from the Thelyphron tale.

Third, the wounding of Thrasyllus in the eyes may be read as mirroring Thrasyllus' piercing of Tlepolemus' right thigh with his lance in the hunt narrative. Thrasyllus takes aim when his companion has begged for help in staving off the attacks of the ferocious boar (8.5). In this context, Charite takes Thrasyllus' place in the episode of the boar-hunt and lures him into entering her home (and, by extension, her plot); Thrasyllus takes the position earlier reserved for his victim; the wine serves as the remote equvalent of the horse that Tlepolemus rides; and the sharp hairpin becomes a substitute for the lance that fatally wounds Tlepolemus. The major difference between the schemes devised by Thrasyllus and Charite lie in the distinct objects: the former is attempting to kill his rival, making his death appear the doing of the boar, whereas the latter blinds her opponent in retribution for killing her husband and planning to marry her.

Finally, Thrasyllus' punishment may be seen as re-enacting the boar's fatal injury of Tlepolemus with its piercing tusks. Support for this interpretation is lent by the earlier representation of Charite as an animal and, by extension, the human equivalent of the boar in the trickery of the hunt. In 8.8, Charite turns down Thrasyllus' marriage proposal by uttering 'animal-like moans,' *ferinos mugitus*; in 8.11, she bursts into the room to punish Thrasyllus like a raging beast, *fremens invadit*. Taken together, these two features evoke the description of the boar, appearing from its lair and blazing with a savage mouth: *impetu saevo frementis oris totus fulmineus* (8.4). In this context, the sharp hairpin serves as a substitute for the boar's pointed tusks.

The similarity between the boar and Charite is also intended to disclose a stark contrast between them: seemingly, the boar kills its enemy outright, although Tlepolemus' death is the result of Thrasyllus' role in the hunt. On the other hand Charite disables her enemy horrifically while allowing him to live, believing that this is *worse* punishment than taking his life at once, and ending all his worldly woes. A necessary element of revenge is that the victim be forced to suffer the 'poetic justice' of the retribution exacted on him. It is not enough that he dies: he must also suffer from the realization of his crime. Thus Charite's mirroring of Thrasyllus' actions emphasizes the notion that she is paying her opponent back with the same coin for all his crimes: both the one against her husband and the one against herself.

The severe pain of the wounds awakens Thrasyllus from his drunken stupor. This signals the dispelling of any illusion of marrying Charite, who now carries her role as faithful widow to its conclusion. She takes her husband's sword and rushes in a frenzied state to his tomb to kill herself, as she has previously sworn to do in her angry speech over the sleeping Thrasyllus (8.12). The townspeople try unsuccessfully to prevent her from committing suicide. Their failure to remove the sword from her hands contrasts with her relatives' earlier success in preventing her from dying at Tlepolemus' funeral. Charite now delivers a speech in which she discourages the bystanders from weeping (8.13):

> 'abicite,' inquit, 'importunas lacrimas, abicite luctum meis virtutibus alienum. vindicavi in mei mariti cruentum peremptorem, punita sum funestum mearum nuptiarum praedonem. iam tempus est, ut isto gladio deorsum ad meum Tlepolemum viam quaeram.'

> 'Stop your tears: they are untimely! Stop your mourning: it is ill suited to my courageous deeds! I have taken vengeance on my husband's bloody killer; I have punished the deadly plunderer of my marriage. It is now time for me to seek with this sword a path down to my Tlepolemus.'

In this speech Charite explains that her husband appeared to her in a dream and illuminated the circumstances of his death. She has since exacted proper revenge on her enemy, Thrasyllus, whom she identifies as both murderer of her husband and destroyer of her marriage.[130] She then states her resolve to take the road to death using Tlepolemus' sword—a sign of her conjugal faithfulness—so that she can extend her union with her lawful husband even into death.

The description of Charite's tragic death in her role as devoted widow represents a 'correction' of the earlier perverted use

---

[130] Charite's speech to the bystanders calls to mind Psyche's courageous address to the mourning relatives in the procession to the rock where she is to be wedded to the beast-husband of Apollo's oracle (4.34). The similarity, however, points up a strong narratological contrast: Psyche's address reveals the triumph of illusion, as created by Apollo's oracle, that she is going to be wedded to a beast-husband.

of wedding imagery in the scheme of her clandestine marriage to Thrasyllus. Suicide on his tomb using his sword may be read as symbolizing the consummation of the couple's 'marriage' in death. From a Freudian perspective, the phallic significance of the sword is easily apparent.[131] Moreover, Charite's self-wounding with Tlepolemus' sword in her right breast may be interpreted as sexual intercourse;[132] the sepulcher may be taken as the figurative analogue of the marriage bed; the outpouring of blood caused by Tlepolemus' sword stands for the deflowering of the bride on the wedding night: *in suo sibi pervolutata sanguine* (8.14). This symbolic (re)union takes place in public, as befits an honorable wedding, in contrast to Charite's clandestine pseudo-marriage to Thrasyllus. Such a reading is also in keeping with the subsequent acts of Charite's friends: they wash her body as part of the funeral rites and then bury her in the same grave as her husband, so as to reunite the couple forever in death: *corpus ablutum unita sepultura ibidem marito perpetuam coniugem reddidere* (8.14).

Structurally speaking, the marital imagery at this point strikes a parallel with Tlepolemus' earlier liberation of his abducted bride from captivity and their subsequent marriage. The earlier narrative contains a web of allusions to Roman wedding rites, and we have seen that Charite's punishment of Thrasyllus is similarly represented. The above structural analogy is further strengthened

---

[131] See Adams 1982, 21.

[132] Charite's self-wounding with Tlepolemus' sword recalls Dido's impaling herself with the sword Aeneas had left behind. A similar argument for Dido's death in Vergil's *Aeneid* 4, which is often cited as a model for the Apuleian tale of Charite, has already been advanced by Moorton Jr. 1990, 163, with bibliography there.

by the fact that Thrasyllus is twice described as a thief, thereby associating him with Charite's abductors, the robbers: first, in 8.1, the narrator compares him to a gang of robbers, *factionibus latronum male sociatus*; and second, in 8.13, Charite herself identifies him literally as *nuptiarum praedo*.

Going still further, we can detect several obvious similarities between the plan enacted by Tlepolemus at the robber's cave and that devised by Charite to rid herself of Thrasyllus. In both cases a friendly guise is adopted and a pretext supplied for the consumption of wine, which is used to overpower the enemy. In this light the Charite plot can be seen as foiling a second abduction, with the captive taking the initiative. The ensuing suicide is to some extent predictable, since it is the only way to bring about the couple's reunion.

When Thrasyllus becomes conscious of Charite's tragic death he rushes to the couple's grave, where he seeks to assuage their angry spirits by entombing himself with them and dying of starvation: *'ultronea vobis, infesti Manes, en adest victima'* (8.14). This death by starvation fulfills Charite's earlier prophesy regarding his marriage to *orbitas*, deprivation: the avenging and angry souls of Tlepolemus and Charite drive Thrasyllus directly to their tomb, thus acting as *pronubae*. His death, figuratively presented as yet another marriage, thematically evokes the death of Charite, who is presented as marrying her ('separated') husband in death. Moreover, as scholars have pointed out, Thrasyllus' self-imposed death is reminiscent of Charite's earlier proposal shortly after

Tlepolemus' funeral (8.7).[133] The feminine manner of Thrasyllus' death by starvation helps to characterize him as a female. This is entirely fitting, for we have already noted that he can be regarded as a victim of emasculation. It is ironic that he should die as such, given his appeal to Tlepolemus' machismo in the hunting narrative. Like Charite, the widowed bride, Thrasyllus seeks consolation in the tomb. However, this similarity also conceals a hidden contrast; whereas she was originally dissuaded by her parents, he succeeds in dying of *inedia*.

In sum, after his failed courtship of Charite, Thrasyllus devises a scheme to kill Tlepolemus in the boar-hunt and marry his widow. This scheme finds its parallel in Charite's clandestine marriage plot, in which she appears to submit to Thrasyllus' proposal so as to take revenge. This plot, like Thrasyllus' trickery before it, involves role-playing and contains imagery evoking the marriage ritual. The imagery continues in the description of Charite's ensuing suicide on her husband's tomb, represented as a (re)marriage to her husband in death, as well as in Thrasyllus' death by starvation in Charite's and Tlepolemus' tomb. Thus, all three characters in the tale, Tlepolemus, Thrasyllus and Charite, meet a tragic death, as their 'marriages' end in disaster, despite the success of their respective schemes. The tragic end to all these 'marriages' highlights the futility of human love in Lucius' adventures as an ass.

---

[133] Hijmans Jr. *et al.* 1985, 139 (s.v. *inedia*), point out that this method of death is used by loving wives. Compare Antigone's death in Sophocles' play of the same name.

CHAPTER III

Unsuccessful Performances

In chapter II we discussed the concept of 'fatally successful performances' in two tales detailing the fate of the avaricious robbers and the lustful Thrasyllus. In this chapter we shall attempt to elucidate the concept of 'unsuccessful performances' by focusing on two more tales: that of the miller's wife (9.14-31) and that of the *noverca* (10.2-12).

In both cases the wives pretend to be faithful, but in fact blatantly disregard their marital vows, thus revealing their true colors. The most striking difference between the two stories lies in their outcome: the miller's wife kills her husband and brings about the sale of the ass to a new master, whereas the wicked stepmother is sentenced to exile for her crimes and her evil slave is condemned to death. This difference is explained by the fact that the miller's wife resorts to a witch to kill her husband, while the stepmother uses poison to murder her stepson.

1. The Ass as Helper?
The Ass' Tale of the Miller's Wife

In 9.14-31 Lucius the ass narrates the tale of the miller's cruel wife, in which he also participates as a character. The woman in question devises a plan to replace her cowardly lover with a new one called Philesitherus. An old maid plays the helper and brings this lover home to have sex with her mistress. The ass, however, exacts revenge on both women by disclosing everything to the miller. In doing so he acts both as an opponent in the plan and as a helper for his master. When the truth is revealed, the miller exacts his own revenge on Philesitherus, who is still a boy, by going to bed with him and then whipping him on his buttocks with a rod. The wife then resorts to a witch and brings about her husband's death. In contrast, the miller's wife and her maid emerge unscathed in spite of their moral laxity.

The ass' inability to comprehend the tragic consequence of his actions is also mirrored in his failure as narrator to understand the events he relates. Before launching into his account, the ass compares his knowledge if not his prudence to that of his literary prototype, the Homeric Odysseus (9.13).[134] He then recounts the tale of the miller's wife, referring to it as 'most delightful beyond any other' (*bonam prae ceteris* 9.14). This is despite the fact that the tale culminates in a tragic ending, which readers may justifiably feel has been brought about by the ass' inept interpretation of events. Yet again, Lucius the ass fails to bear in mind the fact that women are familiar with magic, from which there is no hope of salvation, as his own involvement with Fotis has made clear. For all his claim of having accumulated knowledge, the protagonist displays a remarkably consistent inability to learn from his misadventures.

While scholars have often observed affiliations between the tale of the miller's wife and the adultery mime,[135] or have noted the

---

[134] For the affinities of Lucius' wanderings with those of Odysseus, see Harrison 1990, 193-201.

[135] Schlam 1992, 77, outlines the characteristic elements of the adultery mime; Bechtle 1995, 107, also defines the tale as mime. Winkler 1985, 15-16, observes that the entire tale presents a variation of the adultery theme, acted out by the same cast of characters. For a discussion of the tale, see Mattiacci 1996, 14-21.

presence of vocabulary borrowed from the stage,[136] I focus on the constant shifting of roles by all major characters in the narrative.

In the tale, the ass informs his audience that the miller was a good man, but had the misfortune to be married to a lustful wife. Her shameful conduct went beyond debauchery; she appeared to derive pleasure from persecuting the ass daily with extreme malice (9.15), perhaps out of jealousy for the bond of trust between the animal and his master.

The ass becomes curious about the wife's sex life when he discovers an illicit lover visiting her bedchamber. To his frustration he is unable to identify the man because of the *velamentum* over his eyes (9.15), a covering which serves to hide the wife's adultery while revealing her shrewdness. The wife has an old maid with whom she daily concocts schemes to bring about the miller's downfall.[137] The ass defines these plots using the theatrical term *scaenae* (*scaenas fraudulentas* 9.15).[138] Lucius' long asinine ears are his only consolation in his sorrowful transformation, because they allow him to overhear conversations between the two women even from a distance.[139] His overt curiosity anticipates the plan he later hatches to exact revenge on the miller's wife both for dishonoring her marriage and maltreating him.

In the first conversation Lucius overhears between the women, the old maid expresses her disapproval of her mistress'

---

[136] Hijmans Jr. *et al.* 1995, 148 (s.v. *scaenas fraudulentas construebat*), also 387.
[137] Hijmans Jr. *et al.* 1995, 147 (s.v. *adulterorum internuntia*), views the old maid as a typical *lena* of mimes.
[138] See above n. 136.
[139] See Winkler 1985, 150.

current lover for being terrified of her husband. On the other hand, she praises the adulterer Philesitherus (9.16):

> '[d]e isto quidem, mi erilis, tecum ipsa videris, quem sine meo consilio pigrum et formidulosum familiarem istum sortita es, qui insuavis et odiosi mariti tui caperratum supercilium ignaviter perhorrescit ac per hoc amoris languidi desidia tuos volentes amplexus discruciat. quanto melior Philesitherus adulescens et formonsus et liberalis et strenuus et contra maritorum inefficaces diligentias constantissimus! dignus hercules solus omnium matronarum deliciis perfrui, dignus solus coronam auream capite gestare vel ob unicum istud, quod nunc nuper in quendam zelotypum maritum eximio studio commentus est.'

> 'You must decide yourself, mistress, what is to be done with this feeble craven lover you acquired without my advice, who shudders like a coward at the wrinkle of an eyebrow from your unpleasant, disagreeable husband, and who as a result tortures your willing arms by the slothfulness of his languid loving. How much better Philesitherus would be! He is young, handsome, engaging, vigorous, and fearlessly persistent in the face of the futile precautions of husbands. By Hercules, he alone deserves to enjoy the favours of married women; he alone deserves to wear on his head the golden crown, if for no other reason than the extraordinarily skilful way he recently tricked a certain jealous husband.'

The image of the golden crown, signifying military achievement, helps to cast Philesitherus into the role of an elegiac *miles amator*, as he is interested in sexual rather than military conquests.[140] The

---

[140] Hijmans Jr. *et al.* 1995, 155-56 (s.v. *coronam auream*), observe that the golden crown points to a triumph. On the basis of this association, these commentators draw a parallel between Philesitherus and *Hercules Invictus*. On the other hand, Westerbring 1978, 71, notes in 9.20 a possible parody of Ovid *Am.* 1.9.1: *militat omnis amans et habet sua castra Cupido.*

maid then recounts the narrative of the brave lover's exploits (9.16-21).

In the maid's tale, the decurion Barbarus entrusts the chastity of his wife to a slave named Myrmex before leaving on a business trip. Philesitherus sees Barbarus' wife, whose very name, *Arete*, casts her as a paragon of virtue, and gains access to her bedchamber by bribing Myrmex. The husband returns home just as the lovers are about to fornicate.[141] Philesitherus hears Barbarus entering the house and quickly puts on his clothes, but forgets his sandals. As the master rushes to his room, Myrmex leads Philesitherus unnoticed out of the house. The following day Barbarus finds the stranger's sandals under his bed and becomes suspicious of his wife. In his rage he orders two other slaves to drag Myrmex in shackles to the forum. On the way there they chance upon Philesitherus, who instantly remembers the sandals and accuses Myrmex of stealing them from the baths.[142] The accusation is so much in keeping with the slave's protestations of innocence that Philesitherus cleverly outwits the jealous Barbarus (9.21).

In relating the tale of Philesitherus' exploits, the old woman appears in the same position as the principal narrator, Lucius the ass, who recounts the tale for his own audience, both fictive and actual. Yet unlike the ass, who is an eyewitness to his narrative, the maid possesses only hearsay knowledge of her story. This

---

[141] This unexpected homecoming anticipates the miller's early arrival in the narrative frame, given the thematic interconnections between the two tales.

[142] Kenney 1998, 250, observes that the theft of clothes from bathers was a common crime.

difference can be seen to explain the ensuing failure of the plan of the miller's wife.

On hearing the tale, the mistress characterizes Barbarus' wife as *beata* for enjoying the company of Philesitherus, while identifying herself as *misella*, because her own lover is even afraid of the ass. Ironically, the lover's fears are entirely justifiable in view of the ass' ability to overhear the conversation of the two women from a distance.[143] The maid then promises to bring Philesitherus home to her mistress later that evening.

In the actantial structure, the actor/character administration may appear as follows: the miller's wife takes the position of the subject as maker of the plan, her object/value being to acquire the seemingly intrepid Philesitherus as a lover. The wife also appears in the receiver position; the maid plays the helper; finally, both the ass and the miller are opponents.

The maid's departure to bring the adulterer home signals the commencement of the plan. The wife takes advantage of the miller's absence at a dinner party, and prepares her own luxurious dinner to welcome her new lover. At around noon the ass is released from his yoke, a detail which coincides with the removal of the veil from the lover's face. The presence in the narrative of the verb of seeing, *prospectare*, emphasizes the eyewitness nature of the ass' description of the adulterer and his antics (9.22):

> puer admodum et adhuc lubrico genarum splendore conspicuus, adhuc adulteros ipse delectans.
>
> He was no more than a boy, still conspicuous for the smooth brightness of his cheeks, still attracting male lovers.

---

[143] Hijmans Jr. *et al.* 1995, 194 (s.v. *scabiosi asini faciem timentem familiarem*).

Such a description differs considerably from the maid's earlier portrayal of Philesitherus as a resourceful and brave youth worthy to enjoy all married women.[144] In addition, it anticipates the lover's far from intrepid behavior when the miller returns, and the revenge exacted on him once the ass reveals his presence in the house.

As Philesitherus is sipping some wine the husband unexpectedly returns, just as Barbarus did in the maid's tale. Yet this structural similarity is intended to direct attention to a contrast between the two husbands. The miller's wife expresses the wish that her husband break both his legs and then hides her lover under a grain tub. Seen from an intratextual perspective, this feature forms a parallel with the 'Tale of the Tub' (9.5-7), in which an adulterous wife conceals her lover in a tub. Philesitherus' hiding signals the abrupt end of the wife's plan (9.16-21). At this point she assumes the role of chaste spouse and seeks to discover the reason for her husband's early homecoming. Her subsequent curiosity to know more about the affair of the fuller's wife prompts her husband to recount yet another tale.

In the ensuing narrative the fuller's ostensibly unimpeachable wife falls in love with a suitor, thus signaling her assumption of a new role as unfaithful spouse. The illicit couple are entwined when the fuller brings his friend the miller home for dinner. To avoid detection the lover hides under a basket containing sulfur,[145] the fumes from which prove his undoing. On hearing someone sneeze

---

[144] van Mal-Maeder 1995, 115-16, comments on the element of surprise, which results from the ass' characterization of Philesitherus as *puer*.

[145] This situation is clearly meant to tally with the main narrative, as Philesitherus is hiding under a grain tub near the dinner table at which the miller relates the fuller's tale.

loudly several times, the fuller lifts the basket and discovers the lover close to death from asphyxiation. In a fit of rage the cuckold tries to kill his rival with a sword, but the miller prevents him from doing so by arguing that the paramour will eventually die from the deadly sulfur. The miller also persuades the unfaithful wife to spend a few days at a female friend's house, to allow time for her husband's anger to abate. Here the miller assumes the role of a 'civilized' husband, in complete contrast to his subsequent behavior at home.[146] The similarities between the miller's story and the frame-tale make the former a paradigm for the latter. The miller, however, fails to perceive these connections and thus discover the full implications of his tale.

In her role as chaste spouse, the miller's wife keeps on calling the fuller's wife unfaithful so as to conceal her own immorality; she even proposes that the woman be burned alive for dishonoring her sex. At the same time she repeatedly urges her husband to retire to bed, because she is desperate to free her own lover from the tub. There is more than a hint of irony in what ensues: having left his friend's house in disgust and without eating, the miller forces his wife to serve him the meal which she had prepared for her lover, thus foreshadowing his assumption of the role of *amator* himself (9.26).[147]

---

[146] Hijmans Jr. *et al.* 1995, 387, observe that "the pistor as known by outsiders is one persona, as known by his wife is another."

[147] In structural terms, the two second-hand tales, one told by the old maid and the other by the miller, before the exposure of the adultery of the miller's wife, may evoke the pattern of two tales, one told by Aristomenes and the other by Thelyphron, before the incident of Lucius' transformation into an animal.

The turning point in the evening's events occurs when Lucius finds the opportunity he has been seeking to exact revenge on the miller's wife for her outrageously hypocritical behavior. While being led out to water by a lame stableman,[148] the ass sees the young lover's fingers sticking out from under the basket and tramples on them. Philesitherus' screams of pain exposes the wife's adultery plot.[149]

The narrative relating the ensuing punishment of Philesitherus artfully recreates the crime of adultery originally planned by the miller's wife. Firstly, by revealing Philesitherus to his master, the ass mirrors the behavior of the old crone who brought the same man home to have sex with her mistress. Secondly, the miller assures the pale and trembling adulterer that he has nothing to fear (9.27): *'[n]ihil triste de me tibi, fili, metuas.'* The lover's reaction contrasts with the crone's claims in 9.16, when she portrayed Philesitherus as so fearless of husbands that he deserved to be favored by all married women: *contra maritorum inefficaces diligentias constantissimus!*[150] Thirdly, having claimed in 9.27 that he

---

[148] On the theme of lameness in this episode and that of Aristomenes, see Paschalis 1992, 125. Moreover, the ass likens the lover under the tub to a tortoise. As this animal is notoriously slow in movement, it foreshadows the lover's inability to escape punishment for his crime, unlike the maid's earlier narrative of his exploits (9.16-21). An intratextual reading reveals a connection with Aristomenes' pseudo-metamorphosis into a tortoise when the witches burst into the room to exact their vengeance on the sleeping Socrates (1.12).

[149] The ass-narrator again defines this plan using the theatrical term *scaena* (9.27). Moreover, in revealing the presence of the adulterer to his master, the ass contrasts with the slave Myrmex, who disobeys his master's orders and lets the lover in and out of the house unseen.

[150] Scholars (e.g. Tatum 1969, 520-21; Bechtle 1995, 112-13 and 116) have often discussed the antithesis between the miller's reaction and that of the two husbands in each of the two embedded tales. The husband's calm address to the

always shares everything with his wife (*nam et ipse semper cum mea coniuge tam concorditer vixi, ut ex secta prudentium eadem nobis ambobus placerent*), the miller marches Philesitherus off to bed, becoming an *amator* himself. Fourthly, the young man changes into an *amatus*, albeit unwillingly, by becoming the miller's paramour, instead of offering his sexual services to the miller's wife. Finally, the miller excludes his wife from the proceedings by locking her in another room, thus mirroring his own absence when the old crone first brought the adulterer home. Ironically it is the miller rather than his wife who ends up going to bed with the boy.

The next morning, the master summons two of his strongest slaves to lift Philesitherus up. These slaves act as helpers in the revenge plan, just as Lucius before them. Having referred to his wife's would-be lover disdainfully as *puer* (9.28),[151] the miller admonishes him for attempting to play the sexual aggressor, whips him on the buttocks with a rod and throws him out of the house, leaving him to run away in tears: *maerens profugit* (9.28). Notice of divorce is then served on the unfaithful wife; in his role as vengeful husband, the miller takes a much harder line than he did at the fuller's house.

At this point it is worth noting several similarities between the maltreatment of Lucius and the punishment inflicted on Philesitherus. Firstly, before dawn every day the miller's wife has the ass thrashed in her presence (*antelucio ... insistens iubebat incoram sui plagas mihi quam plurimas irrogari* 9.15). In a similar fashion, the

---

lover, however, may be taken as intended to recreate the behavior of his wife when she receives the adulterer in her house.

[151] This characterization of Philesitherus echoes the ass' description of him in 9.22: *puer admodum*.

miller has Philesitherus tied up at first light and then whips him (*cum primum rota solis lucida diem peperit ... ferula nates eius obverberans* 9.28). Secondly, on the day of his arrival at the miller's house the ass is supplied with abundant food (9.11), thus foreshadowing the lover's banquet laid on by the miller's wife (9.22). Finally, after the miller's death the ass is sold to a new master, the market-gardener, just as Philesitherus is thrown out of the house in tears. These similarities may be accounted for if the two characters are viewed as opponents to plans devised by the unfaithful wife and the miller respectively.

The discovery of the adulterer at the mill is a direct result of the ass' intervention. What he fails to bear in mind is that the miller's wife may resort to magic, which he defines as an art well-known to women: *ad familiares feminarum artes* (9.29).[152] The turning point in the miller's fortunes comes about when the cruel wife engages a witch and offers gifts to help either to regain her husband (and, by implication, enable her to continue her immoral life), or to kill him.

In this new plan, the actor/character administration in the actantial structure changes as follows: the wife again appears in the position of the subject as maker of the plan, her object/value being either to reconcile with her husband or have him killed by an evil spirit. Both the witch and later the ghost occupy the helper's place, which was earlier reserved for the old maid. The opponent position can only be filled by the witch if she fails to carry out the wife's orders.

---

[152] Jones 1995, 15, characterizes the miller's wife as a witch.

At the onset of this plan the witch fails to break the husband's spirit. She thus incites the ghost of a violently murdered woman to kill the miller.[153] Her failure to soothe the miller's wrath contrasts with the man himself, who had earlier managed to calm down the fuller. The witch's choice of ghost is understandable, since victims of violent death were considered highly dangerous.[154] Moreover, the figure of an apparently harmless disheveled woman is deliberately calculated to lull the miller into a false sense of security.

In an aside to the main narrative, the ass directly addresses his fictive audience, who he believes may question the credibility of his narrative.[155] The narrator assures his listeners that thanks to his curiosity and his asinine appearance, he was able to discover the plan hatched by the miller's wife and the witch. Yet again, this ability is clearly not combined with an astute mind; at the end of the tale Lucius has still not learned his lesson and is thus condemned to wander further, bringing misfortune both on himself and those he trusts. The ass' actions in the ensuing market-gardener sequence are more than adequate proof of this observation.

---

[153] A discussion of this episode as evidence for Apuleius' interest in demonology both in the *Metamorphoses* and the *De deo Socratis* appears in Habermehl 1996, 138.

[154] Felton 1999, 57.

[155] For discussion, see Winkler 1985, 69-70. Hijmans Jr. *et al.* 1995, 257 (s.v. *sed forsitan lector* ...), observe that this metanarratological element directs attention to the limited perception of the narrator. On the other hand, Sandy 1999, 92, notes that here the narrator "steps off the pages of the novel to underscore the irony of an asinine narrator."

Unsuccessful Performances

The tragic development of events takes place when a mysterious woman arrives at the mill in the middle of the day, dressed in rags and disfigured by emaciation (9.30). In retrospect, the appearance of this woman is a mask designed to win the miller's sympathy and thus bring about his downfall. In structural terms, the repulsiveness of this figure forms a contrast with the handsomeness of Philesitherus.

The encounter between the woman and the miller, culminating in the cruel death of the latter, cleverly re-enacts several themes that originally appeared in the narrative of the miller's revenge on Philesitherus. First of all, the woman looks emaciated and pale (*lurore buxeo macieque foedata* 9.30), thus forming a distant parallel with the pale and trembling lover discovered by the miller (*exsangui pallore trepidantem puerum* 9.27). Secondly, the woman leads the miller to the private space of his bedroom (*in suum sibi cubiculum deducit* 9.30), the very same place where he exacted revenge on the boy (*deducebat ad torum* 9.28). Thirdly, the woman remains in the room with her victim for a long time with the doors shut, thus recalling the miller who lies with the boy in his bedroom and locks his wife in the next room. Fourthly, when the slaves break down the bedroom and find their master hanging from a noose, we may recall the scene where Philesitherus was lifted up to be whipped (9.28). Finally, the miller's hanging represents a feminine way of dying not unlike Philesitherus' figurative death as a brave lover. This skillful repetition of themes renders the second revenge plot a mirror of the first.

The day after the miller's demise his daughter arrives from the neighboring town in mourning. The ghost of her murdered father has appeared in her sleep with the noose around his neck and disclosed her stepmother's infidelity, her resort to witchcraft and his own descent to the underworld. Intratextually, the tale reveals a striking association with the resurrection of the dead husband in the Thelyphron tale (2.21-30).[156] In that instance, an old uncle of the dead appeals to Zatchlas, priest/magician of Isis, to reanimate his nephew and reveal the secret of his death by poisoning. In both narratives, the dead husband is reanimated for a while, and in both the revived man reveals the infidelity of his wife, her resort to witchcraft and her involvement in his death. The husbands only gain a thorough understanding of their wives' true values only after death. The similarities, however, seem designed to direct attention to a stark contrast between the two narratives: the uncle of the dead appeals to Zatchlas to resurrect the dead husband for a while to prove the widow's guilt. On the other hand, the miller's wife resorts to a witch in order to kill her husband and continue her immoral life. This contrast in turn illuminates the difference between the beneficial magic that Zatchlas practices and the destructive powers of the witch.

After the customary ninth-day-memorial of the miller's death, his daughter auctions her father's estate as well as all the animals belonging to him—including the ass, who is sold on to a market-gardener.

In revealing the presence of the adulterer at the mill to his dear master, the ass appears in a position similar to that of the old crone who plays her mistress' helper and furnishes her with a new lover. In her own revenge, the wife resorts to magic and brings about her husband's cruel death as well as the ass' further

---

[156] I owe this idea to John Hilton.

wanderings. In stark contrast to both the miller and the ass, the miller's wife and her maid are not punished for their wicked behavior, perhaps because they have exacted revenge through magic. As we have said, it is the ass who sets in motion the whole disastrous chain of events. The ass' failure to understand his own role as participant is also reflected in his reference to the narrative as most delightful beyond any other, despite the fact that the tale culminates in a tragic ending. The ass fails to learn anything from his adventures, despite his claim of having acquired knowledge, if not prudence, similar to his literary prototype, the Homeric Odysseus.

2. The Tale of the Stepmother as a Variant of Thelyphron's Tale

Book 10 opens with the arrival of the ass and the soldier in a small town, where they seek refuge in the house of a decurion. The soldier hands over the ass to the decurion's slave and goes to report to his own officers. The disaster which strikes the new host a few days later is the subject matter of this section; the fact that the ass deems the tale worthy of inclusion in the Book constitutes a metanarrative comment on its literary value. As narrator the ass defines the tale as tragedy, perhaps because it largely follows the plot of a *Phaedra* story (*tragoediam, non fabulam legere* 10.2).[157] In actual fact, the similarities between the earlier tale of Thelyphron

---

[157] Tatum 1969, 521.

and the present one of the *noverca*[158] strongly encourage us to consider the latter not so much a tragedy as a variant of the former.[159]

Scholars have devoted considerable attention to the tale's affinities to its literary models. Thus Finkelpearl illuminates the function of verbal echoes from Vergil's *Dido* and Seneca's *Phaedra* in the tale.[160] Following a different approach, Zimmerman draws attention to affiliations with Euripides' *Hippolytus*, and observes that "the actors of this 'tragedy' either are not capable of living up to their 'tragic' role, or even appear to consciously resist that role, and so to step 'out of character'!"[161] For my part, I propose to examine how the tale, coming as it does from the 'alien' literary tradition of a *Phaedra* story, is slowly turned into a variant of the Thelyphron tale (2.21-30), and how this transformation creates a shift in the roles of almost all the major characters.[162] In defining the *noverca* story as a tragedy and therefore as different from the other (comic) tales in the novel, the ass as narrator reveals his inability to exercise authorial control over his own narrative.[163]

---

[158] We should note here the obvious difference between the stepmother, who poisons her lover in order to maintain the appearance of a faithful wife, and the widow, who poisons her husband for the sake of her adulterer and then tries to play the role of the bereaved spouse.

[159] Tatum 1969, 521, observes that when the ass identifies this tale as a tragedy, he reveals the same inability to interpret events as he did when characterizing the adultery tale of the miller's wife as 'most pleasant' (9.14).

[160] Finkelpearl 1998, 149-183. See also briefly Walsh 1970, 171.

[161] Zimmerman 1999, 123; Zimmerman 2000, 442-43. Some similarities with Euripides' *Hippolytus* are also observed by Tatum 1969, 521, n. 70.

[162] Walsh 1970, 172, n. 1, mentions the use of poison in both the tale of the stepmother and that of Thelyphron, but does not observe other similarities between the two stories.

[163] See also Tatum 1969, 521.

In the early stages of the tale, the narrator describes the woman as being externally beautiful but morally ugly, while her stepson is viewed as a model of reverence and modesty. The stepmother falls in love with her stepson, but pretends to be sick in order to mask her shameful behavior. The ass boasts of his superiority over doctors by reason of his ability to diagnose the stepmother's love-sickness, perhaps from his own personal experience with Fotis: *medicorum ignarae mentes* (10.2).[164] There is an element of irony, however, for in the latter part of the tale an actual doctor puts an end to the stepmother's murderous plans and thus gives a happy ending to the tale.

Following the exposure of her sickness by the ass, the stepmother calls her stepson to her room and confesses her feelings for him (10.3), thus signaling the execution of her plan. She implores the stepson to cure her love-sickness using medical vocabulary: *medela ipsa et salus unica mihi tute ipse es* (10.3). For the sake of appearances the stepmother guarantees secrecy, and justifies her appeal on the grounds that her stepson is the only 'doctor' who can 'cure' her of love-sickness.

The stepson is horrified by these revelations, but in order to avoid angering his stepmother he pretends that he will agree to make love when his father is away. The stepmother hastens to send her husband away to their country estate in order to be alone with the object of her desire, but he keeps finding excuses so as not to keep his promise. This avoidance of incestuous advances

---

[164] For Apuleius' play on Vergil's *Aen.* 4.64-66, see Schlam 1992, 78; Finkelpearl 1998, 165-66. Zimmerman 2000, 78, discerns behind this reference authorial intention to establish the superiority of the narrator over the characters/actors in his story.

triggers the stepmother's transformation from a *Phaedra* figure into a heinous character;[165] she decides to silence the stepson for good by resorting to poison. A corrupt slave is sent to a doctor to procure the necessary potion. This solution recalls the widow in the Thelyphron tale who poisoned her husband to gain his inheritance and live with her adulterer. In terms of motive it is also reminiscent of the tale related by Aristomenes, in which the witch Meroe decides to kill her lover Socrates for attempting to abandon her. The stepmother's resort to poison, however, communicates a pattern of action markedly different from that of the witch Meroe, and in retrospect helps explain the exposure of her plan. The earlier representation of the stepson as a figurative doctor conditions the slave's choice of turning to a physician rather than a witch to buy the poison.

The stepmother's intentions develop into a plan. In terms of actantial structure, the actor stepmother appears in the position of the sender; the stepson from an object of the stepmother's desire turns into the object of her hatred; the slave occupies the place of the subject; both the doctor and his poison occupy the helper's position. Within this structure, the opponent position is left empty.

The plan develops contrary to expectations when the stepmother's own son comes home from school and assumes a role not designated for him. He drinks the poisoned wine intended for his stepbrother, and thus unwittingly occupies the hitherto vacant opponent position. This unpredictable and unintentional

---

[165] Zimmerman 1999, 124, observes here that the stepmother "ceases to be a tragic Phaedra, and emerges as the wicked and poisoning stepmother who is a stock character of rhetorical declamations."

interference, caused by a self-positioned actor, triggers the undoing of the entire plan. Yet, rather than showing any remorse over her son's death, the stepmother concocts a cover-up plan in order to maintain appearances as faithful wife.[166] The stepmother then sends a messenger to her husband and informs him of the tragic events. Upon his return, the stepmother accuses her stepson of the murder, claiming that he committed the crime because *she* rejected *his* sexual advances (10.5):

> ac mox eodem ocius ab itinere regresso personata nimia temeritate insimulat privigni veneno filium suum interceptum. et hoc quidem non adeo mentiebatur, quod iam destinatam iuveni mortem praevenisset puer, sed fratrem iuniorem fingebat ideo privigni scelere peremptum, quod eius probrosae libidini, qua se comprimere temptaverat, noluisset succumbere. nec tam inmanibus contenta mendacis addebat sibi quoque ob detectum flagitium eundem illum gladium comminari.

> [A]nd he soon returned in haste from his trip. Then, playing her part with extreme audacity, she pretended that her own son had been poisoned by her stepson. Indeed this was not a total lie, seeing that the younger boy had anticipated the death prescribed for the older one. But she claimed that her stepson had murdered his younger brother because she had refused to succumb to the stepson's shameful lust when he had tried to seduce her. Not content with these monstrous lies, she added that he had even threatened her too with a sword for revealing his crime.

---

[166] The devising of a scheme to conceal shameful conduct calls to mind the widow in the Thelyphron tale. Despite having poisoned her husband, she played the role of model wife all along. The plan to hire a guard was part of her attempt to make this role convincing.

There is an element of ironic truth in the stepmother's claim that her stepson has caused the death of his half-brother; the latter has actually died in place of the former. The remaining accusations against the stepson (that he initially tried to seduce her and then threatened to kill her should she divulge the crime) invert fictional truth in two ways: first, the stepmother was the one who tried to lure her stepson into her chamber; second, she is now the one attempting to silence him by bringing false accusations against him to his father.

Like his younger son who had earlier mistaken the poisoned wine for a wholesome drink, the husband is completely fooled by appearances and fails to investigate his wife's charges. Thus after the funeral he goes to the authorities and begs them to punish his son. The father's courtroom tears move those present so much that they call for the son to be stoned to death, but the magistrates insist they cannot condemn the guilty party without a hearing.[167] The revelation of the *noverca's* crimes during the ensuing trial recalls the exposure of the widow's crime in the funeral procession-cum-trial towards the end of the Thelyphron tale.

In the stepmother's tale the crier calls the plaintiff and the defendant to testify. It is decided that the slave, who asserts that he alone knows what has transpired, should also be called to the stand. It is worth noting that the stepmother herself is absent from court, and that it is the slave who conducts the defense in her place. In his testimony, the wicked slave plays the faithful servant and accuses the stepson of summoning him in anger over the stepmother's scorn, and asking him to give the poison to the

---

[167] Schlam 1992, 79, notes that this is the only story in the *Metamorphoses* in which the responsibility of the magistrates serves justice.

younger brother. Since the stepbrother suspected that the slave would not give the poison to the younger brother, but keep it as future evidence against him, he is said to have administered the poison to his younger brother in person (10.7). The slave's testimony removes all doubt in court and the stepson is duly sentenced to death. In accordance with the procedure followed in such cases, the sentence must be approved by vote before it can be carried out.

At this point a physician intervenes, and in his testimony reveals that the slave came to him several days earlier to buy poison for a sick man, to help him commit euthanasia. In the slave's pretext for buying the poison, the son was portrayed as a sick man about to die from an incurable disease, thus echoing the stepmother who had presented herself as dying from love-sickness. The cunning doctor had suspected the crime and protected himself against future accusations by asking the slave to put the coins in a bag with his seal on it, so that the gold could allegedly be examined by a banker the following day. The fact that the physician happens to be a respected decurion lends all the more weight to his testimony. When he sees the slave in court, the physician sends an unspecified person to bring the gold and defend his innocence in the trial.

In revealing information he alone knows, the doctor appears in a position similar to the dead husband in the Thelyphron tale, whom Zatchlas, Isis' priest, briefly brings back to life in order to furnish otherwise unobtainable evidence regarding his demise. The substitution of the stepson is justified by the fact that the doctor alone can unmask those responsible for the son's murder. This doubling of characters is substantiated by the earlier portrayal of the stepson as a figurative doctor.

The stepmother's slave accuses the doctor of lying. These accusations thematically evoke the widow in the Thelyphron tale, who argues with her revived husband about the truth of his testimony in order to save her plot from exposure. The identification of the slave's seal on the bag reveals without any doubt his role in the purchase of the poison. The slave, however, continues to defend his testimony (and therefore the plot of his mistress) even under torture.

At this point the doctor responds to the slave's accusations by disclosing yet another piece of information known only to him: he has substituted the poison with a sleeping potion. Thus, if the boy drank the potion, he must be sleeping and not be dead. The trial stops and the decurions along with the townspeople go to the tomb. The father opens the coffin and sees his son just as he is about to awake from his death-like sleep. The doctor's role in the trial reminds us of the revived husband in the Thelyphron tale who in response to his wife's challenges furnishes conclusive, eyewitness evidence for the mutilation of his guard by the witches during the wake.

In the stepmother's plan to poison her stepson, the doctor moves from the helper's position to that of the opponent, mirroring the stepson who devised various excuses to avoid giving in to his stepmother's sexual designs. This shift of the doctor's position in the actantial structure, itself a form of role-metamorphosis, is facilitated by the fact that in antiquity physicians provided both medicine and poison. A witch might have offered an alternative solution. The 'resurrection' of the 'dead' son reveals the truth of the doctor's testimony and exposes the stepmother's plot to silence her stepson. As a result, the stepmother is sentenced to exile, following the pattern of divorce as established in the adultery tale of the miller's wife in Book 9, while the wicked slave is sentenced to death (see Ch. III.1). Ironically, in maintaining his role to the end, the faithful slave becomes responsible for both his own death and the punishment of his mistress. In all probability, the stepmother's failure to resort to a witch brings about both her own punishment and that of her wicked slave.

The connection between the Thelyphron tale and that of the *noverca* is further highlighted by their respective positions within the novel's narrative: the former is placed after the opening of Book 2, while the latter comes shortly before the end of the penultimate Book.

In the tale of the stepmother, therefore, there are several themes and motifs that originally appear in the Thelyphron tale. In attempting to poison the stepson so as to maintain her image as a faithful wife, the stepmother evokes the widow, who poisoned her husband for the sake of her adulterer, and then devised a scheme to create the illusion of faithfulness. During the trial the doctor furnishes conclusive evidence to expose the stepmother's crimes, just as the re-animated husband in the Thelyphron tale reveals the secret of his death, exposing his wife's guilt. Thus the tale, which comes from the 'alien' tradition of a *Phaedra* story, is slowly transformed into a variant of a previously occurring tale. The transformation of this entire narrative conditions the change of roles by all characters in it. In seeing superficial similarities with the Phaedra tradition, the ass-narrator identifies his tale as a tragedy unlike all the other (comic) tales in the novel. He thus exhibits a lack of authorial control over his own tale and a failure to interpret the events of his narrative correctly.[168]

---

[168] See also Tatum 1969, 521.

CHAPTER IV

Man and Animal

In this chapter I shall attempt to illuminate the concept of humans acting as animals and vice versa by focusing on two distinct tales: (1) the tale of the robber Thrasyleon (4.14-21); and (2) the ass' performance as a human in the possession of Thiasos (10.16-35). Thrasyleon plays the bear even outside the space formally designed for his performance and, ultimately, dies as a beast. By contrast, the ass refuses to perform his act of sex in public, because he fears that the wild beasts in the arena will be let lose and will devour him along with his partner, the mass murderess. Hence, the ass secretly runs away from the theater and ultimately saves his life. This action becomes a prerequisite for his ensuing salvation by Isis later in Book 11.

1. 'Theater' and 'Spectacle:' The Robber's Tale of Thrasyleon

In the robber's tale of Thrasyleon, the bandit assumes the disguise of a bear in the robbers' stratagem to enter the house of the rich Demochares and plunder it.[169] In doing so, the robbers set in motion the events that lead to Demochares' planned *munus gladiatorium*, designed for the removal of criminals from society: the

---

[169] Tatum 1969, 505; also *id.* 1979, 49; Hijmans Jr. *et al.* 1977, 122-23 (s.v. *prorsus bestiam factum*); and Shumate 1996 (a), 66-67.

pursuit of Thrasyleon in the disguise of a bear, first by Demochares' slaves, and then by the savage dogs in the streets, re-enacts the wild beast hunt, *venatio*, and the *obiectio* of criminals *ad bestias*, respectively. Concurrently, his fight for survival, albeit in his animal disguise, evokes the gladiatorial contest of the *munus* proper.[170] Thus Demochares' splendid preparations for his forthcoming *munus gladiatorium* are fulfilled in Thrasyleon's performance of the bear's role, contrary to the prevailing view that these elaborate preparations achieve no result within the tale's action.[171] This reading is facilitated by Thrasyleon's three distinct roles as beast, criminal and gladiator. Moreover, as the three roles succeed one another, so do those of the narrator as participant in the events of his homodiegetic narrative:[172] first, as the scheme's

---

[170] Cf. Habinek 1990, 64-65. Although Habinek points out that Thrasyleon in the final moments of his life re-enacts the three types of spectacle, he assesses the episode differently:

"He is first and foremost an actor, committed to maintaining the *persona* he has adopted. But in his thrust and parry of his combatants through specific schemes and patterns (*variis corporis sui schemis ac motibus*: 4.20) he plays the part of a gladiator who participates in an elaborate patterned series of movements. Finally, in succumbing to the chasing of the dogs and the impaling with spears, Thrasyleon figures as the victim of a *venatio*, a beast hunted and felled before the eyes of all" (p. 64-65).

Most recently, Slater 2000, 110-11, advances the view that Thrasyleon's performance recapitulates two types of amphitheater spectacles: the *venatio* and the *objectio* of criminals *ad bestias*.

[171] Scholars assume that Demochares' elaborate preparations for his planned spectacle are not fulfilled within the tale's action; see, e.g., Habinek 1990, 65:

"[t]he narrator of Thrasyleon's downfall never saw the exhibition Demochares was preparing, but his vivid and sympathetic account of Thrasyleon's performance gives some sense of the informed pleasure he might have derived from it."

[172] For a definition of the term, see Hijmans Jr. *et al.* 1995, 11.

co-author; then as helper when he presents Thrasyleon/bear to Demochares; and finally as opponent when Thrasyleon's performance as bear provides the missing element in Demochares' spectacle and thus sets it in motion within the tale's action.

My object here is to demonstrate Thrasyleon's role changes and how they condition corresponding changes in narratorial role. These shifts result from Thrasyleon's transformation from a bear to a performer in the *munus gladiatorium* put on by Demochares. Thrasyleon dies precisely because he fails to sustain the wild beast disguise and thus exposes his plan.

The Thrasyleon narrative relates the robbers' stratagem to enter the house of the *munerarius* Demochares and plunder it. The robbers arrive at Plataea and hear talk of a rich man who is preparing to produce a public entertainment equal in splendor to his wealth (4.13): *digno fortunae suae splendore publicas voluptates instruebat*. Demochares fulfills the meaning of his name, which is a compound term of the nouns *demos* and *charis*.[173] At the same time he offers a different kind of pleasure to the robbers when they hear rumors of his abundant wealth.

The narrator then describes Demochares' elaborate preparations for his spectacle, in which criminals will be thrown *ad bestias* to be devoured. This feature prefigures the fate of the criminal Thrasyleon when he disguises himself as a bear in order to enter the rich man's house and rob it. Demochares uses his wealth to buy bears, because of the good entertainment which these

---

[173] Forcellini 1965, vol. V, 472 (s.v. *Demochares*).

animals offer the crowd. The removal of these animals from their natural habitat is the cause of their death.[174]

Shortly before the planned gladiatorial spectacle, the bears bought by Demochares are struck down by a mysterious illness, and die. Two robbers—the narrator and Babulus—see several poor people in the streets of Plataea gathering around the carcasses to obtain free meat. They then come up with the plan of selecting the largest bear carcass and using its hide for their stratagem to enter Demochares' house and plunder it. The narrator defines this scheme as clever (*suptile consilium* 4.14), yet attentive readers may well regard it as most foolish, since Demochares is now in desperate need of bears for the production of his splendid *munus*. Structurally speaking, the robbers who eat the bear's meat and prepare its hide appear in the same position as the starving people who were earlier presented as gathering around the carcasses to obtain free edible meat. Far from devouring criminals, the bears end up providing a free meal for both the poor townsfolk and the robbers.

Babulus then disappears from the narrative, presumably because the robbers' stratagem requires a man of action. Details of this *consilium* appear in the oath which the robbers take together (4.14):

> ut unus e numero nostro, non qui corporis adeo, sed animi robore ceteris antistaret, atque is in primis voluntarius, pelle illa contectus ursae subiret effigiem domumque

---

[174] Kyle 1998, 193, observes that "[t]he paucity of meat in the normal diet of the urban plebs probably meant that almost every bit of edible non-human flesh was eaten up."

Man and Animal

> Democharis inlatus per opportuna noctis silentia nobis ianuae faciles praestaret aditus.
>
> '[O]ne of our company, who should outrank his fellows in courage even more than in physical strength, and above all be a volunteer, was to conceal himself in that skin and take on the likeness of a bear; after he had been brought into Demochares' house, he was to take advantage of the still of night and provide us with an easy entrance through the door.'

The plan calls for someone who must possess both physical strength and courage. Above all, he must be a volunteer. In the 'audition' several bandits express a desire to take on the role of the beast, but Thrasyleon is deemed to best fulfill both requirements. It thus appears that his name (Greek for 'daring lion')[175] belies his nature. When he takes the oath, *sacramentum* (4.14), and volunteers to undertake the risk, Thrasyleon appears to be taking the gladiatorial oath (*auctoramentum*) to endure all kinds of punishment and even death by an iron weapon.[176] Gladiators who bound themselves by this oath were professionals and fought in the arena for pay. In this respect, they differed from gladiators who took part in spectacles in order to display their martial prowess.[177] The binding power of Thrasyleon's oath accounts for his conduct at the closing of the tale and also provides an explanation for the narrator's comments on the absence of *fides* in the world, except in the society of robbers (4.21: *nullam fidem in vita nostra repperiri, quod ad manis iam et mortuos odio perfidiae nostrae demigrarit.*) Evidence

---

[175] For this etymological play, see Frangoulidis 1991 (a), 109; Kenney 1998, 232, translates the term as 'lionheart.'

[176] For gladiators and their oath, see Hopkins 1983, 24.

[177] Edmondson 1996, 107.

external to the tale also helps characterize Thrasyleon as gladiator: later in Book 4 the robbers' captive girl, Charite, twice identifies the robbers as gladiators: (1) *horrendum gladiatorum populum* (4.24); and (2) *cum inruptionis subitae gladiatorum fit impetus ad belli faciem saeviens, nudis et infestis mucronibus coruscans* (4.26).

Thrasyleon's performance requires his donning the bear skin and assuming the likeness of the beast (4.15):

> Thrasyleonis caput subire cogimus parvisque respiratui circa nares et oculos datis foraminibus fortissimum socium nostrum prorsus bestiam factum inmittimus caveae modico praestinatae pretio, quam constanti vigore festinus inrepsit ipse.
>
> We forced Thrasyleon's head right up to the edge of the beast's throat through the hollowed-out neck, gave him some small holes around his nose and eyes for breathing, and put our dauntless comrade—totally turned beast—in a cage, which we had purchased beforehand fairly cheap. With resolute vigour he eagerly ambled into it unaided.

The covering of Thrasyleon with the bear's hide may be interpreted as a 'costume.' In his assumption of this role the robber is in fact transformed into a beast: *prorsus bestiam factus* (the particle *prorsus* belongs to the specialized vocabulary that describes metamorphosis).[178] Technically speaking, this metamorphosis becomes possible as the robbers carefully prepare the animal's hide in order to make it look real (4.14). Thrasyleon in fact steps as far as possible into his role by eating bear's meat before he even dresses up as bear. Thrasyleon's transformation, however, blurs the distinction between illusion and fictional reality to the extent that it

---

[178] Habinek 1990, 64-65.

becomes almost impossible to distinguish between the two, notwithstanding the narrator and those of the audience who share his authorial view.

The robbers expand on their scheme. They purchase a cage and put Thrasyleon in it, thus completing his metamorphosis into a beast. They then forge a letter from a Thracian friend of Demochares named Nicanor, and attach it to the cage so as to make the bear appear as a gift. In their scheme, the robbers seem to take advantage of the present situation in every perspective. First, they supply Demochares with a much-needed bear (*nam diutina captivitate fatigatae simul et aestiva flagrantia maceratae, pigra etiam sessione languidae, repentina correptae pestilentia paene ad nullum redivere numerum* 4.14). Secondly, in buying a cage for the wild beast, the robbers appear to mimic those of Demochares' condemned criminals who were earlier presented as building towers to put beasts in for the planned spectacle (*fortissimum socium nostrum prorsus bestiam factum inmittimus caveae modico praestinatae pretio, quam constanti vigore festinus inrepsit ipse* 4.15 ~ *confixiles machinae, subliciae turres structae tabularum nexibus ad instar circumforaneae domus, floridae picturae, decora futurae venationis receptacula* 4.13).[179] Finally, the forged letter ostensibly sent by Nicanor recalls Demochares' other friends, who were previously described as vying among themselves to win favor by sending animals as gifts (*litteras adfingimus, ut venationis suae primitias bonus amicus videretur ornando muneri dedicasse* 4.16 ~ *nam praeter domesticis venationibus captas, praeter largis emptionibus partas*

---

[179] The narrative of the activities of the criminals in Demochares' house is rather complicated; in my reconstruction of the plot sequence I follow the description of the setting offered by Westendorp Boerma and Hijmans Jr. 1974, 409-12.

amicorum etiam donationibus variis certatim oblatas 4.13). This doubling of the tale's plot in the form of a scheme supports the reading of Thrasyleon's performance as a representation of the planned *munus gladiatorium*. The real irony is that the robbers offer Demochares *everything* he needs for the successful production of his spectacle.

In the actantial structure, the actor/character administration may appear as follows: Babulus and the tale's narrator occupy the position of the sender as 'co-authors' of the robbers' scheme. The rest of the robbers may also appear in the place of the sender, since their companions are working on behalf of the entire gang. The receiver position is filled by the gang, given that everyone stands to gain from plundering Demochares' house. Thrasyleon takes the place of the subject, his object being to provide access to the house. The tale's narrator and the robbers who present Thrasyleon/bear to Demochares occupy the helper position. The opponent slot may be filled by Demochares and the rest of his slaves, should they hinder Thrasyleon's performance as a bear. The narrator also comes to occupy the opponent position, when Thrasyleon's performance as bear sets in motion the production of Demochares' gladiatorial spectacle.

The initial part of the scheme is enacted at nightfall so as to avoid detection (4.16). The robbers present the cage with the bear/Thrasyleon to Demochares along with the forged letter. In this context the house acquires the function of an inner stage, upon which Thrasyleon's performance will take place. Demochares fails to detect the danger lurking within the gift; the robbers' stratagem functions as a brilliant parody of Vergil's tale of the

Trojan Horse in *Aeneid* 2, adapted to a new and entirely different literary environment.[180]

Demochares expresses his amazement both at the extraordinary size of the animal and the generosity of his friend, who appears to be consoling him for the loss of all his bears: *qui miratus bestiae magnitudinem suique contubernalis opportuna liberalitate laetatus* (4.16). Thrasyleon's metamorphosis into a beast makes the scheme's detection almost impossible. Demochares orders his slaves to give money to the robbers for the joy they have given him in his time of trouble. At the outset of the tale, Demochares is presented as having spent a large part of his inheritance on obtaining bears: *totis utcumque patrimonii viribus immanis ursae comparabat numerum copiosum* (4.13). The acquisition of a replacement fills the missing element needed for the production of his spectacle, and thus sets it in motion. Such a reading is contrary to the prevailing view that his magnificent preparations for his *munus* do not materialize within the tale's action.[181] Moreover, the reference to Thrace as the bear's place of origin reflects the tendency of *munerarii* to strive for novelty in their shows by introducing animals imported from distant places.[182]

---

[180] See Frangoulidis 1991 (a), 95-111. For parodic resonances of Sinon's speech in Vergil's *Aeneid* 2 and, by extension, the Fall of Troy, not only in the tale of Thrasyleon, but also in *Risus* festival, the plot of Psyche's sisters, and the tale of Tlepolemus/Haemus, see now Finkelpearl 1998, Chs. 2 and 3. For echoes of Vergil and Lucretius, see Graverini 1996, 171-87. For the presence of theatrical elements in Sinon's speech in *Aeneid* 2, see Paschalis 1997, 106-07, who treats the characters appearing in Sinon's speech to the Trojans from the semantic point of view, as 'masks' for Sinon himself.

[181] See above n. 170.

[182] For the similarities between the tales of Thrasyleon and pseudo-Haemus, see Frangoulidis 1994, 337-48.

The acquisition of the false bear by Demochares increases his status as *munerarius*: his fellow-citizens come to see the large animal and praise its owner as *felix* and *beatus* (4.16). This gathering of people is in keeping with the tactic of producers to put their animals on public display before the *munus* proper.[183]

In his role as owner Demochares orders his slaves to take the beast to its park, but the narrator intervenes and advises him to select an open and well-ventilated place within the house (4.17):

> 'quin potius domus tuae patulum ac perflabilem locum, immo et lacu aliquo conterminum refrigerantemque prospicis? an ignoras hoc genus bestiae lucos consitos et specus roridos et fontes amoenos semper incubare?'

> 'Instead why not look around your house for an open, well-ventilated area? Better yet a place next to some pool, which would be cooling. Or don't you know that this type of beast always has its lair in thick groves and moist caves and near pleasant springs?'

This advice takes into consideration the reasons for the loss of the captive bears. They have died from inactivity, heat and the outbreak of an epidemic. Demochares agrees with the suggestion and allows the robbers to put the animal in a cool place of their choice, but turns down their offer to spend the night with the beast, on the grounds that his slaves are experts in feeding bears (4.17):

> '[n]ihil indigemus labore isto vestro,' respondit ille, 'iam paene tota familia per diutinam consuetudinem nutriendis ursis exercitata est.'

---

[183] Wiedemann 1992, 59, points out the posting of inscriptions as forms of advertisement of the novel features in gladiatorial displays.

'There is no need for you to take that trouble,' he answered. 'By now nearly all my staff have had plenty of practice in feeding bears.'

Here there is an element of irony, given that the so-called expert slaves had earlier been unable to prevent the death of the genuine bears. Following this exchange Demochares disappears from the narrative, in stark contrast to the narrator, who is present at the performance and attempts to alter its course when it gets out of hand.

The narrative then describes the activities of the robbers both inside and outside the house. They first withdraw to a neighboring cemetery and prepare the coffins as storage boxes for their booty.[184] Later at night, when everybody in the house is fast asleep, Thrasyleon comes out of the cage, kills the sleeping guards and the doorkeeper, opens the doors and shows his comrades the treasury. At this point Thrasyleon suspends his role as bear in favor of his true nature as thief. The narrator then instructs his accomplices to carry the haul out and put it in their storage boxes. There is more than a hint of irony in the robbers' choice of storage facilities if one considers the violent death awaiting Thrasyleon.

However, the robbers' bear-scheme gives way to that of Demochares' *munus gladiatorium* when Thrasyleon is encouraged to act the wild beast once more, so as to scare off unwanted attention; he gives such a fine performance running riot around the house that he wakes a slave and the alarm is raised. A pack of

---

[184] The sight of the funeral monument evokes the scene of the dead bears, lying all over the streets at Plataea (4.18: *monumentum quoddam conspiciamur procul a via positum* ~ *passim per plateas plurimas cerneres iacere semivivorum corporum ferina naufragia* 4.14).

hunting dogs is unleashed, pursues the bear out of the house and savages him to death in the street.

In the actantial structure, the actors/characters now appear in the following positions: Demochares is the sender; the hunters and the wild dogs are the subject, their object being to catch the wild bear. The house-slaves who run after the bear occupy the helper position, while the narrator acts as opponent. One could perhaps further argue that the receivers are all those who feast their eyes on the bear being torn apart in the street. In this reading Thrasyleon seems to occupy two distinct positions in respective plans and/or plots: (1) as a means to assist the robbers gain access to the house; and (2) as the object of pursuit in what turns out to be the *munus*, which the robbers' scheme inadvertently and indeed ironically sets in motion within the tale's action. This spectacle is composed of a *venatio*, and the *objectio* of criminals *ad bestias*. If it is to be accorded the status of a true *munus*, Thrasyleon's death cannot but occur in the 'open street' (4.20), in front of a 'milling crowd' (4.21), rather than behind closed doors in Demochares' house.

Furthermore, Thrasyleon's performance is typical of Roman spectacles, in that it fulfills the social function of removing criminals from society. In such shows, as Coleman argues, criminals were condemned to mythological performances as the last debt they owed humanity, i.e. to entertain the crowd.[185] The performances offered criminals a unique opportunity to win back the spectators' sympathy, depending on their skill as actors, and thus be given a chance for acquittal. In his performance as a bear,

---

[185] Coleman 1990, 56.

Thrasyleon seems to re-enact the mythological role of Vergil's Trojan Horse, yet he fails to win the sympathy of his audience and thus meets a fatal death.

Like the robbers' earlier scheme, the production of this spectacle takes place late at night. There is a contrast between the massive bear and the slave-boy, *servulus*, who sees the animal running loose in the house. Rather than running for safety as the robbers expected, the boy rouses the entire household. The narrator is so surprised by this reaction that he attributes it to a divine plan (*divinitus* 4.19). Mindful readers may disagree with this interpretation, seeing instead the enactment of Demochares' braggery that all members of his *familia* are experienced in taking care of bears (4.17).

The sequence of events in this *venatio* mirrors the progression of the bear-scheme. The two performances begin in an almost identical way: the tale's narrator and Babulus see corpses of bears lying in the streets at Plataea, while the slave-boy wakes up from the noise and sees the bear running loose in the house. The noise must be considered as one of the 'non-scripted' elements of the robbers' scheme. Furthermore, in both episodes, action takes place immediately after the event: the two robbers inform their comrades about their plan, while the slave-boy wakes up all the members of Demochares' *familia*. These narratological similarities conceal a stark contrast between the two schemes and in turn explain their diametrically opposite outcomes as distinct types of performances within the tale's action. The robbers devise their stratagem and Thrasyleon carries it out *alone*. The slave-boy, on the other hand, attempts to involve all the members of Demochares' *familia* in this *venatio*, even the hunting dogs. This contrast is explained by the difference on a generic level between theater and arena spectacles: the former requires the assumption and performance of a role, while the latter requires the display of pure martial prowess.

Accordingly, all the members of Demochares' household run after the beast with dogs and all kinds of torches and weapons. The light of the torches deprives the robbers of the opportunity to execute their plan in darkness. The audience recalls that the robbers planned their attack on Demochares' house during the moonless hour of the night when everybody was in a deep sleep: *ex disciplina sectae servato noctis inlunio tempore, quo somnus obvious impetu primo corda mortalium validius invadit ac premit* (4.18). The tale's narrator praises Thrasyleon as he attempts to ward off the attacks of the hunting dogs, thus reassuming in full the bear's role (*mire canibus repugnantem* 4.20). He, moreover, comments on his gestures and movements as he tries to maintain the illusion of his role (4.20):[186]

> scaenam denique, quam sponte sumpserat, cum anima retinens nunc fugiens, nunc resistens variis corporis sui schemis ac motibus tandem domo prolapsus est.
>
> As long as he hung on to life, he hung on to the role he had volunteered to play. Sometimes retreating, sometimes making a stand, varying the postures and movements of his body, he finally slipped out of the house.

Thrasyleon's brilliant performance as an animal temporarily helps him to escape from the house: a fact which suggests that his survival depends on his acting skills. However, while this forced

---

[186] Prescott 1911, 348; Hijmans Jr. *et al.* 1977, 151 (s.v. *variis corporis sui schemis ac motibus*); and Shumate 1996 (a), 67.

exit from the house mirrors his earlier release from the cage, it also signals his withdrawal from the space where the performance of his role as animal was expected to take place. In this external space Thrasyleon cannot survive. At this point, the audience calls to mind the sight of the dead bears lying in the streets of Plataea in the tale's earlier part. Thrasyleon is quite literally thrown *ad bestias* when several savage dogs from a neighboring alley join in the hunt, casting him in the same role as Demochares' condemned criminals in the planned *munus*.[187] Such a reading is reinforced by the similarities between Thrasyleon and the criminals, suggesting that the former is a representation of the latter.

In a desperate attempt to save his comrade from the wild dogs, the narrator pretends to be a member of the household and advises the leaders of the hunt to spare such a large and expensive bear: *'et extremum flagitium, magnam et vere pretiosam perdimus bestiam'* (4.20).[188] The elaborate instructions issued for looting the house are highly successful, and even include an exhortation to return for a second load of booty (4.18). Yet outside in the street, beyond the realm of his own stratagem, the narrator appears powerless to act; he comprehensively fails to dissuade the hunt leaders from killing the bear. In the re-enactment of his mythological role, Thrasyleon fails to win over his own attackers, his audience 'on-stage,' and thus dies at their hands.

The final blow is dealt when a tall and strong fellow comes out of the house and throws his spear into the bear's heart, fatally

---

[187] This alley should not be confused with the one appearing on the comic stage; see Hijmans Jr. *et al.* 1977, 153 (s.v. *de proximo angiportu*), who defend this view.

[188] Hijmans Jr. *et al.* 1977, 155 (s.v. *perdimus*).

wounding Thrasyleon. The circumstances of the robber's death meet the definition of a gladiatorial combat which Wiedemann defines "as bringing death to (one of) the combatants; but it can equally be seen as giving a condemned man an opportunity to regain his physical and social life."[189] Furthermore, the man who fatally wounds Thrasyleon is portrayed as tall and strong, like the valiant robber himself, and thus fulfills the gladiatorial rule which holds that a combatant is expected to fight a worthy opponent.[190]

In terms of the tale's intratextuality, Thrasyleon's death with a lance (4.21) evokes his own killing of the two guards and the doorman with a sword after coming out of his cage in order to assist the robbers in entering Demochares' house to rob it (4.18). It may even pre-empt Tlepolemus' death in the incident of the boar hunt, as in both cases we have an encounter with wild beasts but the final blow is dealt by a human. Moreover, in both cases death takes place in the open space. There is an obvious difference as well: Tlepolemus' death occurs in daytime while that of Thrasyleon takes place during the night. This difference may be explained by the fact that Tlepolemus is an honest person unlike Thrasyleon who is a despicable criminal.

Thrasyleon's admirable performance in the last moments of his life earns him the narrator's praise (4.21):

> enimvero Thrasyleon egregium decus nostrae factionis tandem immortalitate digno illo spiritu expugnato magis quam patientia neque clamore ac ne ululatu quidem fidem sacramenti prodidit, sed iam morsibus laceratus ferroque

---

[189] Wiedemann 1992, 120. The reference to the noise in 4.20 may further highlight the full *munus* status.

[190] For the procedure see Wiedemann 1992, 118.

> laniatus obnixo mugitu et ferino fremitu praesentem casum generoso vigore tolerans gloriam sibi reservavit, vitam fato reddidit.
>
> That illustrious pride of our band never betrayed his soldier's oath by crying out or even screaming. Though torn by teeth and ripped with steel, he continued to growl and roar like an animal, as he bore his present misfortune with noble constancy. He won eternal glory for himself, although he surrendered his life to Fate.

In this passage Thrasyleon continues to emit animal growls, behaving like a beast. In doing so, he honors his oath, just like professional gladiators, who bound themselves with an oath and received their wounds without uttering a cry. Moreover, just as gladiators maintained their glory as performers in the arena even after their death, so is Thrasyleon presented here as gaining glory as a performer in the spectacle despite his demise. On the other hand, the same death may also be read as a punishment for the robber's willingness to renounce his human nature and foolishly play the role of a beast. Thrasyleon's death may even foreshadow the fate of the robbers themselves by Tlepolemus given the fact that Thrasyleon is a thief.

Even after Thrasyleon is dead, the illusion of his role is maintained. Later the next morning, a butcher, albeit timidly, approaches the dead animal to collect meat and feed Demochares' wild beasts. In structural terms, the image of the dead Thrasyleon/bear lying in the street calls to mind the dead bears lying all over the streets of Plataea, while the arrival of the butcher evokes the earlier gathering of poor people around the bear carcasses to scavenge meat from them. The butcher cuts into the beast's belly and pulls out the robber from it (4.21): *utero bestiae resecto ursae magnificum despoliavit latronem.* The image here is of a metaphorical birth, reinforced by the fact that the term, *ursa*, is feminine in gender. Thrasyleon's unmasking by being skinned by a butcher for meat reveals an irony, given that the robber himself earlier had a hand in skinning the bear to eat it and then prepare the disguise. Thus, the butcher brings to fulfillment the narrator's earlier reference to the fate of Demochares' condemned criminals, destined to become food for beasts in his planned spectacle (4.13): *generosa illa damnatorum capitum funera*.

In theatrical terms the butcher removes Thrasyleon's mask, exposing his role as an animal, while at the same time identifying the spectacle of the robber's death as a gladiatorial combat of the *munus* proper. In doing so, the butcher also declares the victory of Demochares' spectacle over the robbers' allegedly clever plan. It thus emerges that in volunteering to take on the bear's role in the robbers' scheme, Thrasyleon ironically falls victim to 'robbery,' when the butcher cuts open the animal's hide and removes its contents. Thrasyleon's identity is thus revealed. The exposure of illusion allows the participants in the spectacle to perceive the theatricality of both the bear-scheme and the *munus gladiatorium*, in contrast to the tale's audience, both fictive and actual, who have been able to enjoy them all along as distinct types of performances.

The representation of Thrasyleon's performance as a bear using imagery reminiscent of gladiatorial spectacles supports its interpretation along the lines of Demochares' preparations for his forthcoming *munus*. Hence there is an element of irony in the substitution for Demochares' condemned criminals and their fate, a view which is confirmed by the order of the enacted events. By the Julio-Claudian period, gladiatorial contests were preceded by a *venatio* and the *obiectio* of criminals *ad bestias*,[191] just as Thrasyleon is thrown *ad bestias* after his pursuit by Demochares' slaves and the wild-dogs (*venatio*). In this fashion the full program of a typical *munus gladiatorium* is artfully reproduced in the narrative of Thrasyleon's performance. Clearly, this reading is assisted by Thrasyleon's three distinct roles as beast, criminal, and gladiator. Furthermore, his change of roles in accordance with the demands of the entire performance also conditions the narrator's own change of roles as participant in his own tale: first, as the scheme's co-author; then as helper when he presents the bear to Demochares; and, finally, as opponent when the robbers' scheme has been transformed into Demochares' spectacle. Thus the narrative of the spectacle compensates for the absence of the description of Demochares' *munus*, since the latter has been artfully represented by Thrasyleon's performance as thief and bear.

2. Thiasos and Venus in the Corinthian Theater

In *Metamorphoses* 10.16-35 Lucius relates the last sequence of his adventures as an ass before his rehumanization in the next Book. Thiasos, the ass' new owner, is preparing a gladiatorial spectacle in his quest for the highest municipal office in Corinth, the *duumvir quinquennalis*.[192] The episode of the spectacle is composed of three acts: (i) a choral dance of pretty boys and girls (10.29); (ii) an elaborate pantomime of the Judgment of Paris (10.30-34); and (iii) the planned copulation of the ass with a mass

---

[191] Wiedemann 1992, 55; Edmondson 1996, 77.
[192] For Apuleius' selection of Corinth as the setting for the spectacle, see Mason 1971, 160-65.

murderess who has been sentenced to be thrown *ad bestias* (10.34).[193]

The order of events in the spectacle seems to produce a meaningful sequence, mimetically re-enacting various stages of the marital ritual. The nubile boys and girls who dance the martial pyrrhic may be interpreted in the context of rites of passage marking the transition from puberty to adulthood. The ensuing pantomime of the Judgment of Paris can be read as a betrothal scene, as Venus promises Paris a wife who resembles her in beauty, i.e. Helen.[194] Finally, the intended copulation of the ass with the mass murderess may be said to represent the consummation of marriage in Roman nuptial rites.

There is a stark contrast between the ass and Paris: whereas the ass, like Paris before him, is to be 'betrothed' to the mass murderess, he eventually refuses to 'marry' the convict for carnal pleasure and saves himself by running away from the theater. In retrospect, this refusal to copulate in public and the secret exit from the theater, which also betokens the protagonist's refusal to have sex for carnal pleasure, will bring about an abrupt end to the long chain of misadventures that started with his sexual involvement with the slave Fotis.

To take this reading a step further, we might tentatively claim that the theatrical performances are a cleverly constructed mirror image of Lucius' rites of initiation in the remainder of the novel, and may indeed foreshadow them. In the performances we

---

[193] For the program of a gladiatorial *munus*, see Wiedemann 1992, 55.
[194] James 1987, 238, treats Paris' marriage to Helen as an adultery story; see also Finkelpearl 1991, 227.

have rites of passage followed by divine intervention and then nuptials. One of the most famous classical tales of divine intervention in human affairs, the pantomime of Paris' Judgment, may hint at the appearance of Isis in Book 11. The connection between Venus and Isis becomes stronger as Apuleius portrays the goddess of love in a way that renders her comparable with Isis. Following his exit from the Corinthian theater, the ass arrives at the seashore of Kenchreae, where he appeals to Isis for help. The goddess intervenes and promises to restore him to human form, provided that he leads a celibate life devoted to her service. Lucius' ensuing initiation into the priesthood is represented as a form of 'divine marriage.'[195] This offers Lucius a non-sexual *voluptas*, the religious ecstasy stemming from contemplation of the divine. It thus contrasts both with his planned 'marriage' in the theater, which he feared would end in his spectacular death for the entertainment of the crowd, and with Paris' betrothal to Helen, which was destined to bring destruction on the young man and his great city.

Scholars have interpreted the narrative of the spectacle either as an instance of the ass' moral development,[196] or as an indication of the opposite.[197] I focus instead on the various roles the animal assumes in the final sequence of his adventures, while in the care of Thiasos. In this concluding section the ass acts out the role of a man and performs various human activities which mark distinct stages in the process of his humanization: (1) he eats human food

---

[195] Lateiner 2000, 326.
[196] Walsh 1970, 182; Schlam 1978, 103; and Tatum 1979, 79-80.
[197] Finkelpearl 1991, 233; Zimmerman 1993, 155.

and delicacies; (2) he learns table manners and sign language; and (3) he has sex with a wealthy *matrona* in a room in his master's house. This is the first occasion on which the ass comes close to human behavior during his wanderings[198] and functions as a rehearsal for his forthcoming rehumanization by the grace of Isis in the next Book. In the early stages of his last adventure as an ass, Lucius is cautious not to act in too precociously human a manner, since he fears that this could lead to his being put to death as an ill omen (10.17). Later on he becomes convinced that if he enters the theater he will be devoured by wild beasts along with the mass murderess.

In 10.13, the opening paragraph of the Thiasos sequence, the ass' fortunes change for the better. The swaggering soldier sells him to two slave-brothers, a chef and a confectioner, who need an animal to carry their baking material and equipment. While in their ownership, Lucius exploits a brilliant opportunity to eat human food and delicacies, for he is not as foolish as to confine himself to animal food: *nec enim tam stultus eram tamque vere asinus* (10.13). Thus he shows pride in mental superiority over asses, failing to bear in mind that this behavior will put his life in great danger. Lucius' new grooms begin to suspect him when they notice their food stocks dwindling and the ass getting fatter, while the animal food is left untouched. The consumption of human fare would be impossible if the ass were a true animal in every sense, and demonstrates Lucius' re-assumption of his role as a human being. While secretly observing the ass enjoying a human meal, the two

---

[198] The sadistic boy's accusation in 7.23 that the ass is lusting after women is untrue.

stable hands burst into laughter. They are overheard by their master, Thiasos, whose mirth is unbound when he learns of the incident. He further orders that the door be opened so as to admire the ass consuming human food and delicacies.

The name Thiasos means 'troupe' and is associated with Dionysian rites and, by extension, theater, while asses were often included in Dionysian theatricals.[199] Thiasos orders that the ass be taken to his dining room for a test of his abilities. Despite being completely sated, Lucius tastes all kinds of meats and fish in order to earn favor. Thiasos is astonished by this precocity. He summons his two slaves and gives them four times what they paid for the animal, thus formally becoming his new owner (10.17). The ass is assigned a trainer, who feeds him like a man and teaches him table manners and sign language. This feigned pupilage marks a second stage in the process of Lucius' 'humanization,' more advanced than the previous one. Although the ass was in a position to perform these tricks without coaching, he wants to convey the impression that he has learnt by training. He is well aware that otherwise people may take him for a magician or ill omen and kill him.

The ass' various performances as a quasi-human being make him famous. Thiasos takes him on a journey to Thessaly in order to acquire wild animals and famous gladiators for his forthcoming *munus gladiatorium*. The mention of Thessaly is understandable, as this region was renowned both for its horses and its magnificent public shows: in 1.7, Socrates, a friend of Aristomenes, falls victim to robbers who attack him near Larissa on his way to watch a

---

[199] For the Dionysian associations of Thiasos' name, see Schlam 1970, 483; Hanson 1989, 250.

gladiatorial spectacle: *per transitum spectaculum obiturus*. Later, in 4.13, at Plataea, a gang of robbers makes a failed attempt to enter the house of the *munerarius* Demochares who is preparing to produce a splendid gladiatorial spectacle for the entertainment of the crowd: *munus edituro gladiatorium*.

On the return journey to Corinth, which takes place partly by land and partly by sea, Thiasos decks out the ass with elaborate trappings and rides on him (10.19). Large crowds gather in the town to admire the remarkable animal, thus enabling Thiasos to earn money from public displays of Lucius' talents. Among the crowd there is a rich *matrona* who falls madly in love with the ass. In her insane passion this woman reveals bestial sexual appetites. The trainer has no qualms in prostituting the beast to the *matrona* at a profit (10.19): *at ille nequaquam sollicitus, quidnam posset de me suave provenire*. Thiasos seems here to be taking advantage of the well-known lustfulness which characterizes asses: in Terence's *Eunuchus*, Antipho identifies his friend Chaerea as *asinus* when the latter narrates to him his rape of the girl Pamphila: *te asinum tantum* (598). The ass' intended copulation with the *matrona* points to the final stage of his 'humanization;' this is the first time Lucius is to make love to a woman like a man following the long period of sexual abstinence after his affair with Fotis. The ass fears that he will harm the *matrona* and will then be thrown to the wild beasts in the forthcoming *munus* (10.22): *heu me, qui dirrupta nobili femina bestiis obiectus munus instructurus sim mei domini*. It seems that the coupling with the *matrona* serves as a review of Lucius' entire career: it is bestial and typical of human weakness from every perspective.

Ironically, the ass' successful performance with the *matrona* prompts Thiasos to include him in the *munus*, to perform an act of copulation with a mass murderess (10.23).²⁰⁰ The ensuing long tale of this woman's crimes, her multiple murders and destruction of her entire family explains the substitution of the *matrona* with the convict as the ass' mate. The arena was the formal place for executing criminals or other individuals condemned to be thrown *ad bestias* (10.23-28), and thus the wealthy *matrona* could not possibly appear in a public sex show, despite her promise to come another time at a fee.²⁰¹ The choice of a convicted criminal as new mate, however, once again shows lack of concern for the ass, while also revealing the animal's naiveté in believing that he could benefit from his master's favor. Thiasos is solely concerned with the glory he expects to win from the splendid spectacle he is putting on in his quest for the highest municipal office in Corinth.

The decision to expose the ass in the arena marks a striking reversal in Lucius' fortunes, for which the ass himself is solely responsible. This change aligns with the theme of metamorphosis running through the novel's entire narrative. The ass defines his union with the condemned murderess as *confarreatio*, which is the most solemn form of marriage: *matrimonium confarreaturus* (10.29).²⁰² All the same he is apprehensive of sexual contact with the convict, lest he be polluted and humiliated in public. These concerns reveal

---

²⁰⁰ Habinek 1990, 56-57 interprets the scene of the ass' lovemaking in the arena in the context of *pharmakos* ritual.

²⁰¹ For the tale of the condemned woman's crimes, see Zimmerman 1999, 125-127. See also Winkler 1985, 177, who views the convict as a doublet of the wealthy *matrona*.

²⁰² On *confarreatio* see Treggiari 1991, 21-24. Zimmerman 2000, 350 (s.v. *matrimonium confarraturus*), comments on the bitter irony in the passage, since the narrator employs a term "which indicates the most ceremonious and sacred form of Roman marriage (i.e. *confarreatio*) to allude to the public mating with the murderess that the ass is expected to perform."

the ass' human self inside his animal skin and are in stark contrast to the human characters, who appear shameless in their actions. The ass wants to commit suicide, but he is unable to kill himself because he is deprived of human hands and fingers. The constraints of his role as an animal leave him with no other option but to participate in Thiasos' sex show.

In the actantial structure, the characters in the narrative of the forthcoming spectacle may take the following position: Thiasos appears in the place of the sender, while both he and the community of Corinth occupy the receiver position. The ass is the subject, whose object is to 'marry' the convicted murderess in public before she is thrown *ad bestias*. The enthusiastic crowd who escort the ass to the theater and the people who prepare the ass' marriage-bed occupy the helper's position; the wild beasts fill the place of the opponent.

On the day of the spectacle, an enthusiastic crowd accompanies the ass to the theater. He remains outside the arena grazing on the grass, thus signaling the resumption of his animal role. Through an open gate he is also able to watch the acts that precede his own performance and, moreover, to narrate them for his audience, both internal and external.

The enactment of the spectacle begins with the entrance of a group of pretty boys and girls dancing the pyrrhic in various (military) formations (10.29). The orderly arrangement of these male and female dancers suggests performance, as all dances involve *mimesis*. Besides, the pyrrhic is a martial dance and relates to male and female rites of passage, mimetically dramatizing the crossover from puberty to adulthood.²⁰³ The unexpected appearance of both boys and girls dancing the pyrrhic can be explained by the metaphoric association of the theme of love with war. The sound of the horn signals the end of this choral dance and marks the transition to the second act, the performance of Paris' Judgment (10.30-34).

A wooden mountain and a young shepherd grazing goats help to characterize the scene as Mt. Ida and the youth as Paris (10.30). A young boy arrives on stage representing Mercury and approaches the shepherd. This boy hands an apple to the shepherd, conveying Jupiter's will that this character should play the role of the judge in the ensuing pageantry among the three goddesses.

In the actantial structure, Jupiter appears in the roles of both sender and receiver; Paris fills the place of subject to render his judgment; the three goddesses along with their entourage occupy the helper's place. In this model, the position of the opponent is left empty.

In the enactment of the Judgment, three girls appear on stage along with their companions. These girls act the roles of Juno, Minerva and Venus, all three accompanied by their entourage. In contrast to the other two goddesses, the *mima* who plays Venus appears virtually naked, her only attire being a thin

---

²⁰³ Mason 1978, 1, notes that the pyrrhic is a dance of Greek origin which became popular in Rome. The pyrrhic is associated with rites of passage. On this, see Lonsdale 1993, 139. Also Zimmerman 2000, 362-63 (s.v. *Graecanicam ... pyrricam*) mentions the connection between pyrrhic and initiatory ceremonies, and especially marriage ceremonies, but does not develop this connection any further.

piece of silk to cover her charms, thus symbolizing sexual desire. Juno and Minerva step forward and make their offering to Paris: the former promises royal power and the latter triumphs in war. Then Venus dances gently to the sound of the flutes. As narrator, the ass places special emphasis on Venus' movements and her entourage: a chorus of young boys representing Cupids light the way to the goddess, as if she were going to a wedding feast (10.32): *et velut nuptialis epulas obiturae dominae coruscis praelucabant facibus.* The comparison is apt, as Venus is about to arrange Paris' marriage to Helen in return for a favorable judgment (10.32): *daturam se nuptam Paridi forma praecipuam suique consimilem.*[204] Given that Paris' marriage does not feature in the pantomime, it is logical to assume that the Venus actress is planning to reappear at the nuptial feast following the 'marriage' between the ass and the convict in the next act.[205] This is understandable, as the ass has been portrayed as Paris' other self, having undergone various misadventures within the novel's narrative. Venus' offer to Paris is especially attractive because he is portrayed as an *adulescens* (10.30; also 10.32: *iuvenis*), and, therefore, of marriageable age. Thus Paris eagerly hands over the prize to Venus for the profit of *voluptas*. In the mythic narrative, as we know, Paris subsequently goes to Greece, violates *xenia* and abducts Helen, the wife of Menelaus. This abduction

---

[204] Extra-textual evidence hints at Helen's 'witch-like powers:' in Homer's *Odyssey* 4.220-32, Helen appears to wield magic drugs, a power which she owes to Venus herself. On this see Boyd 1998, 14.

[205] Zimmerman 2000, 386 (s.v. *velut cenas nuptiales obiturae dominae*) considers the allusion to the wedding as evocative. She cites all passages in the novel where Venus is associated with marriage and treats the reference in the pantomime of Paris' Judgment as ironical, since Venus will assist Paris in his famous adultery, the abduction of Helen.

points to the reversal of Paris' fortune, marking the onset of the Trojan war and the destruction of his race. Thus love gives place to a destructive war. As an instance of divine intervention in human affairs, the episode of Paris' Judgment may foreshadow Isis' appearance to the ass in the next Book in order to offer him salvation from his hardships.

As narrator, the ass disrupts the narrative and delivers his harsh criticism on judicial corruption (10.33):

> [q]uid ergo miramini, vilissima capita, immo forensia pecora, immo vero togati vulturii, si toti nunc iudices sententias suas pretio nundinantur, cum rerum exordio inter deos et homines agitatum iudicium corruperit gratia, et originalem sententiam magni Iovis consiliis electus iudex rusticanus et opilio lucro libidinis vendiderit, cum totius etiam suae stirpis exitio?

> Why are you so surprised, you cheap ciphers—or should I say sheep of the courts, or better still vultures in togas—if nowadays all jurors hawk their verdicts for a price, since at the world's beginning an adjudication between gods and men was corrupted by beauty's influence, and a country shepherd, chosen judge on the advice of great Jupiter, sold the first verdict for a profit of pleasure, resulting in the destruction of himself and his entire race?

In this passage, the ass traces the origin of judicial corruption to Paris' selling his verdict to Venus in return for carnal pleasure. Scholars have often discussed the analogy between Paris and Lucius' former self: like Paris who gave the prize to Venus, Lucius chose Fotis as his mistress.[206] The connection is reinforced in 2.17, where Lucius compares the beauty of the dancing Fotis to that of

---

[206] Smith 1999, 206; Zimmerman 1993, 150-52; and Schlam 1970, 484.

Venus in the pantomime: *in speciem Veneris.*²⁰⁷ In this sense the pantomime is a reflection of Lucius' former life; but there is an element of irony that has received no comment to date: in delivering his harsh lecture on Paris, the ass fails to mention his own foolishness. At this stage readers know only too well that he chose Fotis as his mistress in order to gain access to magic, and was then changed into an ass.

In what follows the ass cites several mythical and historical *exempla* of unfair judgments against Palamedes, Ajax, and Socrates, respectively.²⁰⁸ All of these cases are entirely unrelated to sex, but are intended to direct attention to the harm brought on by unwise judgments. The narrator fears that members of the audience may object to his indignation as a philosopher, perhaps on the grounds that asses are renowned for their foolishness; in fact Lucius' earlier comment to the same effect only reinforces this view (10.13). Thus he interrupts his aside on the corruption of judges and resumes the narration. In retrospect, the ass' *excursus* on judicial corruption helps to explain his ensuing secret exit from the theater and paves the way for his rehumanization in the following Book.

After the judgment, Juno and Minerva leave the stage in anger, thus making clear their disapproval of Paris' judgment, while also anticipating their own role in the Trojan war after Helen's abduction by Paris (10.34). Consequently, the two goddesses make clear their shift in the actantial structure from that of helper to the

---

[207] Zimmerman 1993, 151-52. She further observes here that: "there is a switch in narrative perspective from the actorial narrator to the auctorial narrator, from the 'experiencing I' (je-narré) to the 'telling I' (je-narrant)" (p. 155).

[208] For the grouping see Schlam 1970, 485-86.

hitherto unoccupied opponent position. Soon a chasm opens up and the stage is sunk, signaling the end of the pantomime performance (10.34).[209]

The third act, the intended marriage of the ass to the convict (10.34) counterbalances the earlier pantomime in almost every detail (10.30-34): the ugly ass is the complete antithesis of the handsome Paris and the condemned and morally ugly murderess the opposite of Venus/Helen. The copulation is the logical sequence of the theme of marital rites, suggesting the consummation of marriage in Roman wedding rites. In 10.34, the ass has ironically characterized this lovemaking in public as an illustrious marriage, *praeclaris nuptiis*. This is set to take place in the theater in the middle of the day, thus striking a telling contrast with the ass' lovemaking to the *matrona*, which had taken place in the private space of his master's rooms at night. Moreover, by arranging the 'marriage' to the convict in the theater, Thiasos appears in the same position as Venus, who earlier promised to marry Paris to a wife who equals her in beauty, i.e. Helen (10.32). Hence Thiasos and Venus play parallel roles, arranging catastrophic marriages for their favorites, the ass and Paris, respectively.

As mentioned above, in 10.29 the ass expresses shame at the prospect of public copulation and sexual contact with the polluted convict. Both these reservations reveal a human self trapped in an animal hide. In 10.35, the ass also confesses his fear that wild

---

[209] Finkelpearl 1991, 266, observes phallic associations in the eruption of wine-saffron from the mountain on the top of the goats and the stage. This explosive overflow of wine-saffron attests to Venus' power.

beasts may be let loose while he and the mass murderess are on the 'marital' bed. Since beasts are unable to distinguish between good and evil, the fear is that he will be devoured along with his spouse to be.[210] This concern is understandable, given the earlier graphic description of how Thrasyleon was savaged to death in the streets while disguised as a bear. The ass has previously copulated unhindered with the morally despicable *matrona* without harming her (10.21-22). At this point the ass takes a conscious decision not to copulate with the mass murderess for fear for his life, and secretly leaves the theater, in an exit already prepared by his *excursus* on Paris' judgment. This flight serves as an indication of judgment and highlights the difference between the ass and Paris, whose carnal desires led to his own destruction and also of his entire race.

Lucius' sorrowful adventures began with his 'marriage' to Fotis, but end with his reluctance to 'marry' the convict for carnal pleasure in the theater. Earlier, on various occasions, the ass has cursed Fotis for changing him into an animal, thus making clear his abandonment of the 'principles' that led to his transformation into a beast of burden.[211] In retrospect, the ass' unwillingness to have sex with the convict constitutes a form of celibacy and a rejection of Paris as a prototype. His exit from the theater and arrival at the port of Kenchreae bring about an abrupt end to the

---

[210] Winkler 1985, 147, notes that "Lucius objects not to the sexual contact as such but to the woman's status as a criminal, to the publicity of the act, and (a little later, at 10.34) to the danger of the wild beasts (stupid *animals!*), who might attack him as well as her."

[211] 3.26, 7.14 and 9.15.

long chain of misadventures, although the ass is completely unaware of this positive development in advance.

Having arrived at Kenchreae the ass prays to Isis to deliver him from his hardships. The goddess intervenes and promises to restore him to human form, but demands devotion, which takes the form of initiation into her rites, in the form of 'holy matrimony.' Lucius' 'marriage' to Isis may be taken as forming a distant parallel to Paris, who marries a woman of unrivalled beauty on the suggestion of Venus. The comparison, however, is designed to reinforce a stark contrast between the ass and Paris: unlike the mythical hero, who is wedded to Helen for carnal pleasures, Lucius' 'marriage' to Isis is associated with celibacy. This 'divine marriage' offers Lucius *voluptas* of a non-sexual kind. It thus contrasts with his planned marriage in the theater, which could only have led to disaster. Thus outside the arena, the ass may finally be seen to fully comprehend the dangers of worldly desires and weaknesses, dangers which are graphically illustrated from the outset of the novel, from the Aristomenes tale onwards (Book 1).

The narrative of the spectacle therefore seems to re-enact by *mimesis* certain stages of adolescent transition and marital rites. In this context, Venus and her promise to marry Paris to Helen appears in the same position as Thiasos, who arranges the ass' 'marriage' to the convict so as to spice up the spectacle. The ass is completely responsible for his change of fortune, as he assumes the role of quasi-human being and performs various human activities, all of which mark distinct stages in the 'rehumanization' process. In the ensuing performance of the pantomime, Paris makes a wrong decision and awards the prize of beauty to Venus in return for carnal pleasures with Helen, thus bringing disaster both on himself and his great city. In the same way, Lucius met his downfall when he chose to involve himself with Fotis so as to gain access to magic. In contrast to Paris, the second time around the ass refuses to 'marry' the convict for *voluptas,* runs away from the theater and arrives at the port of Kenchreae. In retrospect, the unwillingness to copulate with the convict in public suggests the 'death' of Lucius' asinine self, brought on by his earlier 'marriage' to the witch's slave. The ensuing devotion to Isis is the moral opposite of the planned 'union' with the mass murderess, which would inevitably have led to the ass being devoured by the beasts. Thus the narrative of the spectacle, which seems to mimetically re-enact stages of marital rites, appears to foreshadow the spiritual covenant forged between Lucius and Isis, with the associated initiation and promise of celibacy. The narrative of Lucius' early attempts to become a man in asinine form thus serve as a foil to his ensuing physical and spiritual rehumanization in the following Book.

CHAPTER V

Successful Performances: Lucius' Spiritual Journey

The final Book of the novel relates Lucius' anamorphosis in the *Ploiaphesia*, the Spring festival dedicated to Isis, and his subsequent initiation into the rites of Isis and Osiris. In 11.5, the goddess interprets the launching of her new ship as symbolizing the recommencement of navigation after winter.[212]

It has been suggested that the *Ploiaphesia* festival is unrelated to the initiations, which form the main theme of the Book.[213] The protagonist's restoration to human form at the festival and his ensuing initiation into the priesthood mark the end of his sorrowful adventures, as if signaling the 'spring' of his new life.[214] Several themes in the account of the launching feature in the narrative of Lucius' two subsequent initiations, and they underscore Lucius' constant 'rebirth' as an Isiac. This emphasis on

---

[212] The symbolism of Isis' boat in her Spring festival seems to be different from the standard symbolism of the boat in her Autumn festival. In the latter, the boat is identified either with the ship with which Isis travels to Byblos to fetch the body of the dead Osiris, or with the vessel that carries the dead Osiris to the underworld. For fuller discussion, see Griffiths 1975, 40-41, with extensive bibliography.

[213] Griffiths 1975, 32. For an excellent survey of all major approaches to, and interpretations of, Book 11, as well as of the work as a whole, see Ruebel 2000, x-xv (foreword by Steve Nimis).

[214] Bowie 1993, 234, observes the following with regard to Dionysus' journey to Hades in Aristophanes' *Frogs*:
"In Eleusinian and other mystery cults, the journey was a standard image for the process of initiation: wandering, tribulation and uncertainty led to bright lights at the end of the initiatory tunnel."

'rebirth' contrasts sharply with the ass' earlier experiences, most of which emphasized the risk of death. Thus the Spring festival may be interpreted as a convenient metaphor for Lucius' entrance into his new life.

Moreover, the initiations are indicative of integration into the Isis/Osiris fellowship; they contrast with the protagonist's earlier refusal to become a member of the Hypatan community and join the 'fellowship of Laughter' after his own unwitting performance in the Laughter festival. Through her festival, Isis offers Lucius salvation and promises him glory and bliss, unlike the god of Laughter, who made a laughing-stock of him and reduced him to tears.[215]

The striking reversal of Lucius' fortunes begins with his secret exit from the theater at Corinth and his arrival at the port of Kenchreae, one of Isis' cult centers.[216] The ass falls asleep, but suddenly awakes, sees the full moon rising from the sea and senses the presence of a benevolent deity, later recognized as Isis. He then goes to the sea to purify himself, prays to the moon-goddess to restore him to human form and falls back to sleep (11.2). It is in this dreamlike world, between sleep and wakefulness, that his encounter with the goddess takes place.

In response to the ass' prayer, the goddess relates the various names by which she is known and concludes by introducing herself as Isis; in this way she implicitly associates her other

---

[215] A brief but useful discussion of the theatrical aspects of both the Isis festival and the Laughter festival appears in Penwill 1990, 5-6. For the element of theatricality in the *anteludia* and *pompa* of the goddess, see Merkelbach 1995, 275-383.

[216] Sandy 1999, 95, with bibliography.

identities with the world of appearances. Although the goddess of many names, Isis acknowledges only one identity for herself. As a result, her contribution to the ensuing anamorphosis of Lucius reinforces the view that the ass' earlier adventures belong to the realm of deception. Isis promises to deliver Lucius from his hardships during the *Ploiaphesia* the following day, and gives him instructions for his salvation. The image of the goddess of seafaring and healing[217] emerging from the sea, *pelago medio* (11.3), foreshadows her role in the anamorphosis of Lucius at the festival dedicated to the sea. Isis demands Lucius' absolute devotion, which entails celibacy (11.6),[218] and promises him glory and a blissful life even after death if he earns her favor. Divine intervention is understandable at this point, given that the ass has already espoused celibacy in Book 10, by refusing to have sex with the mass murderess in the Corinthian theater. What is more, he unwittingly seeks refuge at Kenchreae, one of the places devoted to Isis. There the ultimate truth is revealed to him in a state of slumber closely resembling a dream, just as Charite before him has learnt of Thrasyllus' perfidy through the appearance of her dead husband in a dream (Book 8).

In the narrative of Lucius' reformation, the actor/character administration in the actantial structure may be arranged as follows: Isis takes the place of the sender; she and the ass appear in

---

[217] Burkert 1987, 15.

[218] Isis' epiphany to the ass at night, offering him instructions for his salvation, functions as a form of 'incubation,' a temple sleep, during which patients have dream-visions or receive instructions for their cure. Lucius' illness is his 'asshood,' both literally and figuratively, which Isis promises to cure during her own festival as goddess of healing.

the receiver position. The ass is also the subject, his goal/value being to regain his human form. The priest who hands the wreath of roses to the ass acts as helper. The ass can only fill the position of the opponent if he refuses to carry out Isis' instructions. In this case man and god have identical aims, unlike the structures in previous Books, in which each character had a distinct objective; symmetry between the human and the divine reveals uniformity in the world in which Isis rules.

The following morning the ass faithfully executes Isis' orders. He awakes from sleep and purifies himself with seawater: *marino rore respersus* (11.7). The prevailing atmosphere of renewal on the day of the Spring festival foreshadows the ass' own rebirth (11.7). In the *anteludia*, a carnival procession that precedes the *pompa* of the great goddess, several figures and animals appear in comic disguises, representing other professions or animals (11.8). The contrast between these figures, who assume new roles by changing costumes, and the ass, who remains transformed into an animal through Fotis' magic, reveals the vast difference between the positive magic of Isis and the destructive magic of Fotis, from which there is no hope for deliverance without divine help. In the *pompa* proper (11.9-11), the ass recognizes his savior priest, later identified as Mithras—he carries the wreath of roses, the antidote to Lucius' metamorphosis, as Isis has earlier explained (11.6). The ass approaches, eats the roses and sheds his animal form. This is the cure earlier suggested by Fotis, yet Lucius is unable to obtain it without divine guidance.[219] The rehumanization constitutes a new

---

[219] Schlam 1992, 116. Mention of roses has already appeared earlier in 10.29, but with a reminder that they are not yet in full blossom.

role, as Lucius becomes a completely new person, both physically and spiritually (*renatus* 11.16).

The crowd expresses its awe at Isis' miracle. To a religious audience, the rehumanization may evoke the theme of Osiris' resurrection by Isis in several ways. First, in his adventures as an ass, Lucius appears to have gone through an ordeal similar to that of the god.[220] In 11.6, Isis relates to Lucius that his appearance as an ass is most hateful to her because of the ass' association with her opponent Seth-Typhon: *detestabilis beluae*.[221] Then the relatives and friends, who rush joyfully to see Lucius after his reformation and regard him as having come back from the dead (*reducemque ab inferis* 11.18), help characterize his return to the world of the humans as a 'resurrection.'

Lucius himself is unable to find proper words to thank the goddess, yet he is saved from this awkward position by Mithras, who speaks both to him and on his behalf. In his sermon, the priest metaphorically likens Lucius' land adventures to a dangerous voyage in rough weather, and his coming to Kenchreae to a safe arrival in the port (11.15):

> '[m]ultis et variis exanclatis laboribus magnisque Fortunae tempestatibus et maximis actus procellis ad portum Quietis et aram Misericordiae tandem, Luci, venisti.'

> 'You have endured many different toils and been driven by Fortune's great tempests and mighty storm winds; but finally, Lucius, you have reached the harbour of Peace and the altar of Mercy.'

---

[220] Merkelbach 1995, 266-303, interprets Lucius' animal ordeals as reflecting the experiences of candidates in their initiation into the Isiac mysteries.

[221] Griffiths 1975, 162 (s.v. *mihique ... detestabilis*).

This representation of the ass' adventures on land as a sea voyage may underscore the interpretation of the launching ceremony in fair weather as a visual symbol of, and a metaphor for, the 'journey' of his new life.[222] This metaphor is foreshadowed in 10.19, where the ass' journey from Thessaly to Corinth is described as taking place partly on land and partly by sea. The priest assures Lucius that he has now entered Isis' domain, and urges him to join the *pompa* for the dedicatory launching, so that the unbelievers can recognize their error. According to the priest, Lucius' induction to Isis' service, *servitium*, will offer him greater protection and the opportunity to enjoy the rewards of his freedom: *cum coeperis deae servire, tunc magis senties fructum tuae libertatis* (11.15).

The ceremony itself may be interpreted as a representation and metaphor for Lucius' entrance into his new life. The fact that the anamorphosis takes place at Isis' Spring festival may justify such an interpretation. First of all, the purification of the ship to ensure a fair sailing (11.16) recalls the ass and his ablutions (11.7). In 11.23, Mithras again purifies Lucius with water before initiating him into Isis' priesthood: *purissime circumrorans abluit.* Second, Lucius' 'rebirth' coincides with Isis' festival, figuratively marking the 'death' of his old life. Later, in 11.21, Mithras explains to Lucius that initiation involves a kind of death and rebirth, granted

---

[222] The change of weather at sea is heralded by Lucius' safe arrival at the port of Kenchreae, following his secret exit from the Corinthian theater. It is further consonant with Lucius' physical and spiritual anamorphosis. Similarly, in Homer's *Odyssey*, Odysseus, after the hardships he has experienced at sea when sailing from Scheria, has an easy journey with fair winds. This change of weather runs parallel to Odysseus' (internal) change from the man of the *apologoi*, to the more Odyssean side of his persona. For Lucius' self-comparison with Odysseus, see Ch. III.1.

by Isis' mercy: *ipsamque traditionem ad instar voluntariae mortis et precariae salutis celebrari*. Taken together, these two references may help to establish an association with the sailing of Isis' ship, which marks the end of Winter and heralds the beginning of Spring. Third, the gleaming sail of the ship (11.16) foreshadows Lucius' appearance following his initiation in full glory in front of the crowd, dressed in his Olympian *stola*, like the sun-god Osiris (*ad instar Solis exornato me* 11.24). This is the point at which Lucius fulfills the actual meaning of his name, which derives from the term *lux*, meaning light. Fourth, the prayers repeated by the crowd to ensure a fair voyage echo the story they later relate about the 'pious' life that has earned Lucius divine favor (11.16). Fifth, the flowery appearance of the ship (*carina ... perpolita florebat* 11.16) evokes the wreath of roses eaten by the ass to regain human form. Sixth, Mithras' consecration of the ship to Isis (*deae nuncupavit dedicavitque* 11.16), replicates his earlier exhortation to Lucius to dedicate himself to Isis' service: *obsequio religionis nostrae dedica* (11.15). Later, in 11.19, the goddess herself appears in Lucius' dreams and urges him to seek initiation into her rites: *crebris imperiis sacris suis me, iam dudum destinatum, nunc saltem censebat initiari*. Seventh, the participants in the festival load various offerings onto the ship before it sails away: *muneribus largis* (11.16). This action foreshadows the gifts that Lucius receives from friends, relatives and family slaves upon their hearing the joyful news of his reappearance: *varie quisque munerabundi* (11.18). In 11.23 Lucius again receives various gifts before his admission into the temple and his 'journey' to the threshold of Proserpina, where he comes in contact with both chthonic and celestial gods: *variis quisque me muneribus honorantes*. Thus Lucius' entrance into his new life, culminating in his ensuing initiation into Isis' priesthood, may be seen as a distant equivalent to the sailing of Isis' new ship. Lucius passes from one stage of life and enters a new one; it is as if his life's tribulations on land come to an end in the 'sea voyage' of initiation. The narrative of the Spring festival not only advances the novel's plot but also places Lucius' larger experience within the context of his spiritual journey, making it in some sense its duplicate.[223]

Lucius' integration into the Isiac fellowship is set in direct opposition to his earlier refusal to integrate into the Hypatan community (3.11). During the Laughter festival, the god had given Lucius sorrows and reduced him to tears, whereas now Isis offers him joy and the prospect of a happy life under her protection. Moreover, Lucius never sought the god of Laughter, while he delivers his pious prayer to Isis for salvation shortly after his arrival at the port of Kenchreae, which marks the end of his tribulations (11.2).

Lucius celebrates his new role as a priest with ritual fasting. In this new role Lucius experiences a non-sexual *voluptas*, the religious ecstasy derived from gazing at Isis' statue (11.24; also

---

[223] In Plato's *Phaedo* 58a-b, Phaedo explains the rite which dictated that the Athenians annually send a ship to Delos in fulfillment of their vow to Apollo, in return for his granting a safe return for the fourteen boys and girls sent as a sacrifice to the Minotaur in Crete. These boys and girls constituted the annual tribute of the Athenians to Knossos (on the myth see Rowe 1993, 109). The rite dramatized how Theseus, himself one of the fourteen youths, saved the lives of these boys and girls. It began with the priest of Apollo crowning the stern of the ship, just as in the Apuleian passage the priest Mithras crowns the stern of Isis' ship.

11.25).²²⁴ The initiation into the priesthood may be interpreted as a form of divine marriage based on celibacy,²²⁵ which in itself constitutes a form of emasculation. The earlier comparison of Lucius (11.24) to the sun god Osiris suggests his own pairing with Isis, the moon goddess.²²⁶ His 'marriage' to Isis reinforces the contrast with his earlier attachment to the lowly slave girl Fotis, which brought about his metamorphosis into an ass and the ensuing misadventures. The 'marriage' to Isis also forms a parallel with the divine marriage between Cupid and Psyche on Mt. Olympus, in the central tale of the *Metamorphoses*, often seen as a leading guide on how to interpret the novel's framing narrative.²²⁷

---

²²⁴ A similar kind of *voluptas* brought on by viewing an artifact appears in Pliny the Elder (*NH* 36.4.20-21). In Pliny's story many people sail to Cnidos to view the famous statue of Venus by Praxiteles: *quam ut viderent, multi navigaverunt Cnidum*. Lucius' likening himself to a statue (*in vicem simulacri* 11.24) for the crowd to gaze at reverses the image of his earlier gazing at Isis' statue (11.19). This also contrasts with his earlier rejection of the Hypatan magistrates' offer to cast his image in bronze, as a reward for his unwitting performance in the Laughter festival; that statue would only have served as a painful reminder of having quite literally played the fool. (On this see Winkler 1985, 172.) Finally, whereas in Hypata Lucius turns into an ass after his refusal to integrate into the Hypatan community, here he first regains his human form and then joins the Isiac fellowship. This integration takes the form of successive initiations.

²²⁵ In the narrative of Lucius' initiation into Isis' priesthood, Lateiner 2000, 326, skillfully brings out imagery and vocabulary that allude to the ceremony of Roman wedding rites.

²²⁶ Papaioannou, *per litteras*.

²²⁷ For a discussion of Psyche's rite of passage in the tale of Cupid and Psyche, see Roubelaki (forthcoming). Moreover, Lucius' 'divine marriage' to Isis seems to offer an alternative turn to the standardized plots of the Greek romances in which the separated couple is eventually reunited. In this way the narrative of the *Metamorphoses* appears to be in fruitful 'dialogue' with the Greek romances, altering and redeveloping their conventions. On the genre of the *Metamorphoses*, see Schlam 1992, Ch. 2.

Following a short visit to his hometown, Lucius receives instructions from Isis herself to travel to Rome. He hastily gathers his luggage and sails away: *raptim constrictis sarcinulis, nave conscensa, Romam versus profectionem dirigo* (11.26). The earlier sailing of Isis' ship, which marks the navigability of the seas, foreshadows Lucius' journey to Rome. It further develops the imagery of the metaphorical journey of rebirth into a literal one. Moreover, just as the *Ploiaphesia* ship is associated with trade and, therefore, profit, so Lucius' sailing to Rome anticipates the rich rewards that await him there as a result of his integration into the cult.

For an entire year Lucius fulfills his duties to Isis in the temple of Campus Martius in Rome, regarding himself as fully initiated. Yet, in a dream apparition he receives a call for a second initiation. The protagonist's amazement at this new call reveals a lack of perception similar to that which typified him as an ass. Soon, however, he finds out that he has only been admitted to the cult of Isis and not that of Osiris, which entails further dedication. Osiris even forces Lucius to sell his clothes to obtain money for his initiation.

Critics have often interpreted the emphasis on the costliness of repeated initiations into cults as irreligious and parodic.[228] The enforced penury may however be interpreted as an ordeal in the broad sense of the term, to be endured by Lucius if he is to enjoy the rewards as an Isiac. The selling of clothes also has a symbolic significance, whereby Lucius' old garments represent the 'costume' of his previous self. Furthermore, just as the first initiation into the priesthood rendered Lucius a figurative 'consort' of Isis, the

---

[228] van Mal-Maeder 1997, 104-05 and *passim*; Harrison 2000, 245.

second one may be said to make him 'brother' to Osiris. Thus Lucius assumes the new role of an Osiris-figure in the dual sense, as 'consort'/'brother' of Isis. On the other hand, the continuous, in-depth delving into mystic rites seems to trigger Lucius' eloquence; as a result he successfully practices his career as orator in law-courts and even earns a small profit.

After his second initiation Lucius receives a divine call for yet another, a fact which makes him suspicious of the priests for allegedly failing to do their duty. In a dream apparition, however, Isis intervenes and explains to him that the third initiation is a sign of divine favor; it is necessary because he forgot his Olympian *stola* at Kenchreae and thus cannot perform his service to her. Lucius' eagerness to travel to Rome may explain his forgetfulness.

In Book 11 Lucius constantly receives divine guidance in the form of dreams, all of which explain to him how to understand phenomena. The intermittent presence of Isis and Osiris in Lucius' new life serves to further highlight the absence of similar assistance in the world of the hero's earlier adventures as an ass. The income he earns with heaven-sent help from his practice as a lawyer helps him to alleviate the cost of his initiation. Furthermore, Osiris appears in person in Lucius' sleep and urges him to continue his legal career without fear of his opponents. This new role recalls the only other instance in the novel in which Lucius unwittingly performed as an orator: the Laughter festival at Hypata. However, whereas in Hypata he became an object of ridicule, in Rome he earns both fame and fortune from his work as a lawyer in the forum.

Osiris even elects Lucius to the sacred college of the *pastophori*, an appointment that constitutes an extension of his earlier role as priest. Advancement on both the religious and social levels emerges as a direct result of Lucius' entrance into his new life, just as the earlier sailing of Isis' ship is associated with trade and profit.

Certain scholars have interpreted the final image of Lucius' proud demonstration of his shaven head everywhere he goes as comic.[229] Others have pointed out that the Isiacs were often the target of ridicule and satire for their credulity and naiveté.[230] Lucius' ostentatious display of his baldness, however, may be read along the lines of progressive self-assertion of his new identity as an Isiac priest, and therefore as different from other lawyers in the forum. Moreover, whatever sense of comedy may be noted here, it differs considerably from that in the Laughter festival. As an Isiac Lucius belongs to a religious fellowship that may often be the target of ridicule as a whole, unlike the community of Hypata, in which he *alone* was the victim of cruel laughter, like Thelyphron before him.

Anything but unrelated to the theme of Lucius' initiations, the *Ploiaphesia* may thus be viewed as a metaphor for the protagonist's anamorphosis and entrance into a new life. This transformation culminates with the initiation into the priesthood of Isis. The repetition of themes from the *Ploiaphesia* narrative in Lucius' additional two initiations reinforces the notion of his constant rebirth as a devotee of Isis. Having undergone various ordeals on land, the protagonist finally finds peace in his own 'sea voyage,' which also coincides with the festival marking the seasonal

---

[229] See e.g. Winkler 1985, 224-27.
[230] van Mal-Maeder 1997, 105-06.

navigability of the seas and the transport of goods. As a neophyte Lucius enjoys both religious and social recognition. The successful performance of his role as *mystes* in his various initiations marks his full integration into the Isiac fellowship, in direct contrast to his earlier refusal to integrate into the Hypatan community and their 'fellowship of Laughter.' The reason for this is that the god of Laughter offers Lucius sorrows, unlike Isis who grants him joy and the prospect of a happy life both during his lifetime and after death.

In the narrative of the *Metamorphoses*, therefore, almost all the characters/actors assume roles or engage in performances. More specifically, in the first sequence detailing Lucius' travels before his transformation into an ass, the various characters become caught up in unwitting performances, mainly as a result of the intervention of magic, which humans cannot comprehend and thus guard themselves against. However, in the sequence following Lucius' metamorphosis into an ass, the emphasis of the narrative falls mainly on human relationships and less on magic. In this sequence disguise and deception play a dominant role, since humans are unable to effect transformations in the way witches can. The constant shifting of roles by almost all major characters ties neatly in with the novel's key theme of metamorphosis. Moreover, these roles often mirror one another, thus exposing the polymorphism associated with a world of appearances. In addition, most of the characters who assume roles are punished in the end for compromising their *mores*. The only truly successful performances are those of Lucius as a devotee in the sequence following his anamorphosis. Hence the narrative of Lucius' misadventures highlights the impossibility of finding joy outside the uniform world of Isis.

As far as actantial structure is concerned, in the narrative of Lucius' adventures, including his ordeals subsequent to the transformation into an ass, the clash between opposing roles and plans is extremely prominent. Following the anamorphosis, the absence of any opponents or struggle between Lucius the neophyte and his divine protectors is reflected in the lack of conflicting actantial structures and therefore of conflict. This is how tension is resolved in the final book of the work.

BIBLIOGRAPHY

Adams, J.N. 1982. *The Latin Sexual Vocabulary*. Baltimore and London: The Johns Hopkins University Press.

Anderson, G. 1976. *Studies in Lucian's Comic Fiction*. Leiden: Brill.

Bajoni, Grazia M. 1990. "La scena comica dell'irrazionale (Petr., 61-63 e Apul., *Met.*, I. 6-19 e II 21-30)." *Latomus* 49: 148-153.

Barrett, C. 1994. "The Marriages of Charite and Psyche in the Context of Apuleius' *Metamorphoses*." *CB* 70: 73-88.

Bartalucci, A. 1988. "Considerazioni sulla festa del 'Deus Risus' nelle *Metamorfosi* di Apuleio (2,31-3,18)." *CCC* 9: 51-65.

Bechtle, G. 1995. "The Adultery-Tales in the Ninth Book of Apuleius' *Metamorphoses*." *Hermes* 123: 106-116.

Borghini, A. 1991. "Il platano e la morte: a proposito di Apul. *Met.* 1.19." *Aufidus* 15: 7-14.

Bowie, M.A. 1993. *Aristophanes: Myth, Ritual and Comedy*. Cambridge: Cambridge University Press.

Boyd, T.W. 1998. "Recognizing Helen." *ICS* 23: 1-18.

Bradley, K. 1998. "Contending with Conversion: Reflections on the Reformation of Lucius the Ass." *Phoenix* 52: 315-334.

———— 2000. "Animalizing the Slave: The Truth of Fiction." *JRS* 40: 110-125.

Bruneau, Philippe. 1961. "Isis Pélagia à Délos." *BCH* 85: 435-446.

Burkert, W. 1985. *Greek Religion*. Cambridge, Mass.: Harvard University Press.

―――― 1987. *Ancient Mystery Cults*. Cambridge, Mass.: Harvard University Press.

Calame, Claude 1995. *The Craft of Poetic Speech in Ancient Greece*. Ithaca: Cornell University Press.

Coleman, K.M. 1990. "Fatal Charades: Roman Executions Staged as Mythological Enactments." *JRS* 80: 44-73.

DeFilippo, J.G. 1990. "*Curiositas* and the Platonism of Apuleius' *Golden Ass*." *AJP* 111: 471-492.

Deroux, C. (ed.) 1992. *Studies in Latin Literature and Roman History VI*. Brussels: Collection Latomus 217.

Devereux, G. 1973. "The Self-Blinding of Oedipous in Sophocles' *Oidipous Tyrannos*." *JHS* 93: 36-49.

Dillery, J. 1999. "Aesop, Isis, and the Heliconian Muses." *CP* 94: 268-280.

Dowden, K. 1993. "The Unity of Apuleius' Eighth Book & the Danger of Beasts." *GCN* 5: 91-109.

―――― 1997. *Religion and the Romans*. Bristol: Bristol Classical Press.

―――― 1998. "Cupid & Psyche: A Question of the Vision in Apuleius." In: Zimmerman *et al*. 1-22.

Drake, G. 2000. "Apuleius' Tales Within Tales in the *Golden Ass*." In: Wright and Holloway. 3-27.

Edmondson, J.C. 1996. "Dynamic Arenas: Gladiatorial Presentations in the City of Rome and the Construction of Roman Society during the Early Empire." In: Slater. 69-112.

Elam, Keir 1980. *The Semiotics of Theatre and Drama*. London and New York: Methuen.

Evans-Grubbs, J. 1995. *Law and Family in Late Antiquity. The Emperor Constantine's Marriage Legislation Law.* Oxford: Clarendon Press.

Felton, D. 1999. *Haunted Greece and Rome. Ghost Stories From Classical Antiquity.* Austin: University of Texas Press.

Fick-Michel, N. 1991. *Art et mystique dans les* Métamorphoses *d'Apulée.* Paris: CNRS.

Finkelpearl, E.D. 1986. *The Metamorphosis of Language in Apuleius'* Metamorphoses. Ph.D. Diss. Cambridge, Mass: Harvard University.

―――― 1991. "The Judgement of Lucius: Apuleius, *Metamorphoses* 10.29-34." *ClAnt* 10: 221-236.

―――― 1998. *The Metamorphosis of Language in Apuleius: A Study of Allusion in the Novel.* Ann Arbor: The University of Michigan Press.

Forbes, C. 1943. "Charite and Dido." *CW* 37: 39-40.

Forcellini, A. 1965. *Lexicon totius Latinitatis.* Vols V-VI. Patavii: Typis Aldinianis.

Frangoulidis, S.A. 1991 (a). "Vergil's Tale of the Trojan Horse in Apuleius' Robber-Tale of Thrasyleon." *PP* 46: 95-111.

―――― 1991 (b). "*Charite dulcissima*: A Note on the Nameless Charite." *Mnemosyne* 44: 387-394.

―――― 1992 (a). "Epic Inversion in the Tale of Tlepolemus/Haemus." *Mnemosyne* 45: 60-74.

―――― 1992 (b). "Charite's Literary Models: Vergil's Dido and Homer's Odysseus." In: Deroux. 435-450.

―――― 1994. "Self-Imitation in Apuleius' Tale of Tlepolemus/Haemus and Thrasyleon." *Mnemosyne* 47: 337-348.

_____ 1996. "Wedding Imagery in Apuleius' Tale of Tlepolemus/Haemus." *A&R* 41: 196-202.

_____ 1997. *Handlung und Nebenhandlung. Theater, Metatheater und Gattungsbewusstsein in der römischen Komödie.* Stuttgart: Metzler.

_____ 1999 (a). "*Scaena feralium nuptiarum:* Wedding Imagery in Apuleius' Tale of Charite (*Met.* 8,1-14)." *AJP* 120: 601-619.

_____ 1999 (b). "Theatre and Spectacle in Apuleius' Tale of the Robber Thrasyleon (*Met.* 4.13-21). " In: Zimmermann. 113-135.

_____ 1999 (c). "*Cui videbor veri similia proferens vera?:* Aristomenes and the Witches in Apuleius' Tale of Aristomenes." *CJ* 94: 375-91.

Geffcken, K.A. 1973. *Comedy in the* Pro Caelio. Leiden: Brill.

van Gennep, A. 1960. *The Rites of Passage.* Translated by M.B. Vizedom and G.L. Caffee. Chicago: The University of Chicago Press.

Gianotti, G.F. 1995. "In viaggio con l'Asino." In: Rosa and Zambon. 107-132.

Godwin, J. (ed. and tr.) 1995. *Catullus Poems 61-68.* Warminster: Aris and Phillips.

Gollnick, J.T. 1999. *The Religious Dreamworld of Apuleius'* Metamorphoses. *Recovering a Forgotten Hermeneutic.* Editions SR 25. Waterloo, Ontario: Wilfrid Laurier University Press.

Graverini, L. 1996. "Apuleio, Vergilio e la 'peste di Atena.' Note ad Apul. *Met.* IV 14." *Maia* 48: 171-187.

_____ 1997. "*In historiae specimen* (Apul. *Met.* 8.1-14). Elementi della letteratura storiografica nelle *Metamorfosi* di Apuleio." *Prometheus* 23: 247-278.

_____ 1998. "Memorie virgiliane nelle *Metamorfosi* di Apuleio: Il racconto di Telifrone (II 19-30) e l'assalto del coloni ai servi fuggitivi (VIII 16-18)." *Maia* 50: 123-145.

Greimas, A.J. 1984. *Structural Semantics: An Attempt at a Method*. Translated by D. McDowell, R. Schleifer and A.A. Velie. Lincoln: University of Nebraska Press.

_____ 1988. *Maupassant. The Semiotics of Text: Practical Exercises*. Translated by P. Perron. Amsterdam: Benjamin's.

Greimas, A.J. and J. Courtés 1982. *Semiotics and Language: An Analytical Dictionary*. Translated by L. Crist *et al.* Bloomington: Indiana University Press.

Griffiths, J.G. 1975. *Apuleius of Madauros: The Isis-Book* (Metamorphoses, *Book XI*). *Introduction, Translation and Commentary*. Leiden: Brill.

_____ 1978. "Isis in the *Metamorphoses* of Apuleius." In: Hijmans Jr. and van der Paardt. 141-166.

Gunderson, E. 1996. "The Ideology of the Arena." *ClAnt* 15: 113-149.

Habermehl, P. 1996. "*Quaedam divinae mediae potestates:* Demonology in Apuleius' *De deo Socratis.*" *GCN* 7: 117-142.

Habinek, T.N. 1990. "Lucius' Rite of Passage." *MD* 25: 49-69.

Hanson, J.A. (tr.) 1989. *Apuleius'* Metamorphoses. Loeb Classical Library. Cambridge, Mass.: Harvard University Press.

Harrison, S.J. 1990. "Some Odyssean Scenes in Apuleius' *Metamorphoses.*" *MD* 25: 193-201.

_____ 1997. "From Epic to Novel: Apuleius' *Metamorphoses* and Vergil's *Aeneid.*" *MD* 39: 53-73.

———— 1998. "Some Epic Structures in *Cupid and Psyche*." In: Zimmerman *et al.* 51-68.

———— (ed.) 1999. *Oxford Readings in the Roman Novel*. Oxford: Oxford University Press.

———— 2000. *Apuleius: A Latin Sophist*. Oxford: Oxford University Press.

Heath, J.R. 1982. "Narration and Nutrition in Apuleius' *Metamorphoses*." *Ramus* 11: 57-77.

Helm, R. (ed.) 1992. *Apulei Platonici Madaurensis opera quae supersunt*. Metamorphoseon *libri XI*. Leipzig: Teubner.

Hijmans Jr., B.L. 1986. "Charite Worships Tlepolemus-Liber." *Mnemosyne* 39: 350-364.

Hijmans Jr., B.L. and R.Th. van der Paardt (eds.) 1978. *Aspects of Apuleius' Golden Ass. A Collection of Original Papers*. Groningen: Forsten.

Hijmans Jr., B.L. *et al.* 1977. *Apuleius Madaurensis* Metamorphoses *Book IV. 1-27*. Groningen: Boekhuis.

———— 1981. *Apuleius Madaurensis* Metamorphoses *Book VI. 25-32 and VIII*. Groningen: Boekhuis.

———— 1985. *Apuleius Madaurensis* Metamorphoses *Book VIII. Text, Introduction and Commentary*. Groningen: Forsten.

———— 1995. *Apuleius Madaurensis* Metamorphoses *Book IX*. Groningen: Forsten.

Hofmann, H. (ed.) 1999. *Latin Fiction: The Latin Novel in Context*. London and New York: Routledge.

Hopkins, K. 1983. *Death and Renewal*. Cambridge: Cambridge University Press.

Ian, L. and C. Mayhoff (eds.) 1986. *C. Plinius Secundus. Naturalis Historia*. Volume V. Stuttgart: Teubner.

Ingenkamp, H.G. 1972. "Thelyphron. Zu Apuleius, *Metamorphosen* II 20 ff." *RhM* 115: 337-342.

Jackson, R. 1988. *Doctors and Diseases in the Roman Empire.* London: British Museum Publications.

James, P. 1987. *Unity in Diversity.* Hildesheim-Zürich-New York: Olms.

Jones, F. 1995. "Punishment and the Dual Plan of the World in the *Metamorphoses* of Apuleius." *LCM* 20: 13-19.

Kenney, J.E. 1998. *Apuleius:* The Golden Ass. London: Penguin.

Keulen, W.H. 1997. "Some Legal Themes in Apuleian Context." In: Picone and Zimmermann. 203-230.

────── 2000. "Significant Names in Apuleius: A 'Good Contriver' and His Rival in the Cheese Trade (*Met.* 1,5)." *Mnemosyne* 53: 310-321.

Konstan, D. 1995. "Patrons and Friends." *CP* 90: 328-342.

────── 1996. "Greek Friendship." *AJP* 117: 71-94.

Krabbe, J.K. 1989. *The* Metamorphoses *of Apuleius.* New York: Peter Lang.

Kyle, D.G. 1998. *Spectacles of Death in Ancient Rome.* London and New York: Routledge.

Laird, A. 1990. "Person, 'Persona' and Representation in Apuleius's *Metamorphoses.*" *MD* 25: 129-164.

Lateiner, D. 2000. "Marriage and the Return of Spouses in Apuleius' *Metamorphoses.*" *CJ* 95: 313-332.

LIMC *Lexicon Iconographicum Mythologiae Classicae.* Zürich/München: Artemis, 1981-.

Lonsdale, S. 1993. *Dance and Ritual Play in Greek Religion.* Baltimore and London: The Johns Hopkins University Press.

Mackay, P.A. 1963. "The Tradition of the Tales of Banditry in Apuleius." *G&R* 10: 147-152.

van Mal-Maeder, D. 1995. "L'Ane d'Or ou les *métamorphoses* d'un récit: illustration de la subjectivité humaine." *GCN* 6: 103-125.

_____ 1997. "*Lector, intende: laetaberis.* The Enigma of the Last Book of Apuleius' *Metamorphoses*." *GCN* 8: 87-118.

_____ 1998. *Apulée. Les* Métamorphoses *Livre II, 1-20. Introduction, texte, traduction et commentaire.* Ph.D. Diss. Groningen.

Mason, H.J. 1971. "Lucius at Corinth." *Phoenix* 25: 160-165.

_____ 1978. "*Fabula graecanica:* Apuleius and his Greek Sources." In: Hijmans Jr. and van der Paardt. 1-15.

Mattiacci, S. 1993. "La *Lecti invocatio* di Aristomene: Pluralité di modelli e parodia in Apul. *Met.* i.16." *Maia* 45: 257-267.

_____ (ed.) 1996. *Apuleio. La novelle dell'Adulterio* (Metamorfosi *IX*). Firenze.

_____ 1998. "Neoteric and Elegiac Echoes in the Tale of Cupid and Psyche by Apuleius." In: Zimmerman *et al.* 127-149.

McCreight, Thomas D. 1993. "Sacrificial Ritual in Apuleius' *Metamorphoses*." *GCN* 5: 31-61.

Merkelbach, R. 1995. *Isis regina - Zeus Sarapis. Die griechisch-aegyptische Religion nach den Quellen dargestellt.* Stuttgart-Leipzig: Teubner.

Meyrhofer, C.M. 1975. "On Two Stories in Apuleius." *Antichthon* 9: 68-80.

Moorton, Jr. R.F. 1990. "Love as Death: The Pivoting Metaphor in Vergil's Story of Dido." *CW* 83: 153-166.

Münstermann, H. 1995. *Apuleius*, Metamorphosen *literarischer Vorlagen*. Suttgart: Teubner.

Murgatroyd, P. 2001. "Embedded Narrative in Apuleius' *Metamorphoses* 1.9-10." *MH* 58: 40-46.

Mynors, R.A.B. (ed.) 1958. *C. Valerii Catulli* Carmina. OCT. Oxford: Clarendon Press.

OLD   *Oxford Latin Dictionary*. Edited by P.G.W. Glare. Oxford: Clarendon Press, 1982.

van der Paardt, R. Th. 1971. *L. Apuleius Madaurensis: The Metamorphoses. A Commentary on Book III*. Amsterdam: Hakkert.

────── 1978. "Various Aspects of the Narrative Technique in Apuleius' *Metamorphoses*." In: Hijmans Jr. and van der Paardt. 75-87.

Panayotakis, S. 1998. "On Wine and Nightmares: Apul. *Met.* 1,18." *GCN* 9: 115-129.

Papaioannou, S. 1998. "Charite's Rape, Psyche on the Rock and the Parallel Function of Marriage in Apuleius' *Metamorphoses*." *Mnemosyne* 51: 302-324.

Paschalis, M. 1992. "Philesitherus and Aristomenes." *LCM* 17: 125-126.

────── 1997. *Semantic Relations and Proper Names*. Oxford: Clarendon Press.

Penwill, J.L. 1990. "*Ambages reciprocae:* Reviewing Apuleius' *Metamorphoses*." *Ramus* 19: 1-25.

Perry, B.E. 1967. *The Ancient Romances. A Literary-Historical Account of their Origins*. Berkeley and Los Angeles: University of California Press.

Philippides, S.N. 1984. *A Grammar of Dramatic Technique: The Dramatic Structure of the Carpet Scene in Aeschylus' Agamemnon.* Ph.D. Diss. Irvine.

_____ 1994. "The Narrative Models of A.J. Greimas." *Journal of Literary Semantics* 23: 109-123.

Picone, M. and B. Zimmermann (eds.) 1997. *Der antike Roman und seine mittelalterliche Rezeption.* Basel: Birkhäuser.

Plass, P. 1995. *The Game of Death in Ancient Rome.* Madison: University of Wisconsin Press.

Prescott, H.W. 1911. "*Marginalia* on Apuleius' *Metamorphoses.*" *CP* 6: 345-350.

Prince, G. 1987. *Dictionary of Narratology.* Lincoln: University of Nebraska Press.

Rehm, R. 1994. *Marriage to Death: The Conflation of Wedding and Funeral Rituals in Greek Tragedy.* Princeton: Princeton University Press.

Repath, D.I. 2000. "The Naming of Thrasyllus in Apuleius' *Metamorphoses.*" *CQ* 50: 627-630.

Ricoeur, P. 1989. "Greimas' Narrative Grammar." *New Literary History* 20: 581-608.

Riggsby, A. 1999. *Crime and Community in Ciceronian Rome.* Austin: University of Texas Press.

Robertson, D.S. 1919. "A Greek Carnival." *JHS* 39: 110-115.

Robertson, D.S. (ed.) and P. Vallette (tr.) 1940-45. *Apulée: Les Métamorphoses.* 3 vols. Paris: Les Belles Lettres. (rpr. 1956, 1965, 1971).

Roest, B. and H. Vanstihout 1999. *Aspects of Genre and Type in Pre-Modern Literary Cultures.* Groningen: Styx.

Rosa, F. and F. Zambon (eds.) 1995. *Pothos: Il viaggio, la nostalgia.* Trento.

Rosati, G. 1997. "Racconto e interpretazione: forme e funzioni dell'ironia drammatica nelle *Metamorfosi* di Apuleio." In: Picone and Zimmermann. 107-127.

Roubelaki, A. (forthcoming). "Psyche's Rite of Passage in Apuleius' Tale of Cupid and Psyche."

Rowe, C.J. (ed.) 1993. *Plato:* Phaedo. Cambridge Greek and Latin Classics. Cambridge: Cambridge University Press.

Ruebel, J.M. (ed.) 2000. *Apuleius: The* Metamorphoses *Book 1.* Wauconda, Ill.: Bolchazy-Carducci.

Sanchez, M.R. 2000. "Lucio en el campo: Observaciones sobre los libros VII y VIII del Osno de oro de Apuleyo." *Emerita* 68: 115-139.

Sandy, G.N. 1997. *The Greek World of Apuleius: Apuleius and the Second Sophistic.* Leiden: Brill.

———— 1999. "Apuleius' *Golden Ass:* From Miletus to Egypt." In: Hofmann. 81-102.

Schlam, C.C. 1970. "Platonica in the *Metamorphoses* of Apuleius." *TAPA* 101: 477-487.

———— 1978. "Sex and Sanctity: The Relationship of Male and Female in the *Metamorphoses.*" In: Hijmans Jr. and van der Paardt. 94-105.

———— 1992. *The Metamorphosis of Apuleius. On Making an Ass of Oneself.* Chapel Hill: The Johns Hopkins University Press.

Scobie, A. 1975. *Apuleius* Metamorphoses (Asinus Aureus) *I. A Commentary.* Meisenheim am Glan: Anton Hain.

———— 1978. "The Structure of Apuleius' *Metamorphoses.*" In: Hijmans and van der Paardt. 43-61.

Sharrock, A. and H. Morales (eds.) 2000. *Intratextuality. Greek and Roman Textual Relations.* Oxford: Oxford University Press.

Shumate, N. 1996 (a). *Crisis and Conversion in Apuleius' Metamorphoses.* Ann Arbor: The University of Michigan Press.

―――― 1996 (b). "Darkness Visible: Apuleius Reads Virgil." *GCN* 7: 103-116.

―――― 1999. "Apuleius' *Metamorphoses:* The Inserted Tales." In: Hofmann. 112-125.

Slater, Niall W. 1998. "Passion and Petrification: The Gaze in Apuleius." *CP* 93: 18-48.

―――― 2000. "Spectator and Spectacle in Apuleius." In: Zimmerman *et al.* 110-111.

Slater, W.J. (ed.) 1996. *Roman Theater and Society.* Ann Arbor: The University of Michigan Press.

Smith, W.S. 1989. "Apuleius' Miserly Host and the Transformation of Satire." In: Tatum and Vernazza. 130-131.

―――― 1993. "Interlocking of Themes and Meaning in *The Golden Ass.*" *GCN* 5: 75-89.

―――― 1999. "The Narrative Voice in Apuleius' *Metamorphoses.*" In: Harrison 1999. 195-216.

Takacs, Sarolta A. 1995. *Isis and Sarapis in the Roman World.* Leiden: Brill.

Tatum, J. 1969. "The Tales in Apuleius' *Metamorphoses.*" *TAPA* 100: 487-527.

―――― 1979. *Apuleius and* The Golden Ass. Ithaca and London: Cornell University Press.

Tatum, J. and Gail M. Vernazza (eds.) 1989. *The Ancient Novel: Classical Paradigms and Modern Perspectives.* Hanover, NH: Dartmouth College Press.

Treggiari, S. 1991. *Roman Marriage.* Oxford: Clarendon Press.

Ubersfeld, Anne 1996. *Lire le théatre I.* Paris: Belin.

Walsh, P.G. 1970. *The Roman Novel. The* Satyricon *of Petronius and the* Metamorphoses *of Apuleius.* Cambridge: Cambridge University Press.

Westendorp Boerma, R.E.H. and B.L. Hijmans Jr. 1974. "*Apuleiana Groningana* III." *Mnemosyne* 27: 406-412.

Westerbring, A.G. 1978. "Some Parodies in Apuleius' *Metamorphoses.*" In: Hijmans Jr. and van der Paardt. 63-73.

Wiedemann, T. 1992. *Emperors and Gladiators.* London and New York: Routledge.

Williams, G. 1958. "Some Aspects of Roman Marriage Ceremonies and Ideals." *JRS* 48: 16-29.

Winkler, J.J. 1985. *Auctor & Actor. A Narratological Reading of Apuleius's* Golden Ass. Berkeley & Los Angeles: University of California Press.

Wright, C.S and J.B. Holloway 2000. *Tales Within Tales: Apuleius Through Time.* New York: AMS.

Zimmerman, M. 1993. "Narrative Judgement and Reader Response in Apuleius' *Metamorphoses* 10.29-34: The Pantomime of the Judgement of Paris." *GCN* 5: 143-161.

―――― 1999. "When Phaedra Left the Tragic Stage: Generic Switches in Apuleius' *Metamorphoses.*" In: Roest and Vanstihout. 119-128.

———— 2000. *Apuleius Madaurensis:* Metamorphoses. *Book X. Text, Introduction, Commentary.* Groningen: Forsten.

Zimmerman, M. *et al.* (eds.) 1998. *Aspects of Apuleius'* Golden Ass *II.* Groningen: Forsten.

———— (eds.) 2000. *ICAN 2000: The Ancient Novel in Context.* Groningen.

Zimmermann, B. (ed.) 1999. *Griechisch-römische Komödie und Tragödie III.* Stuttgart: Metzler.

GENERAL INDEX

actant 3, 4, 5
actantial model 3, 4, 22, 52, 85;
    - role 4; - structure 3, 4, 6,
    8-10, 24, 41, 45-46, 74, 76,
    78, 80, 86, 110, 115, 122,
    126, 136, 140, 154-55 155,
    158, 165, 176
actor 4-6, 38 n. 57, 57, 59, 61,
    122-23, 130 n. 170; actor /
    character 5, 7, 10, 22, 41,
    45, 74, 76, 85, 110, 115,
    136, 140, 165; see also
    character
actorial 70, 82, 158 n. 207
Ajax, 63, 158
amator, 112, 114
amatus, 114
anteludia, 164 n. 215, 166
apologoi, 168 n. 222
Apuleius, *Metamorphoses*
    1.5-19 11, 15
    1.6 18-19, 31, 34
    1.7 19, 23, 151
    1.7-10 23
    1.8 20, 23
    1.11 21
    1.12 22-24, 113 n. 148

1.13 24-26, 28, 33
1.14 27
1.16 28
1.17 30
1.19 31-34

2.17 157
2.21 38-39, 45 n. 62, 118,
    120
2.21-30 11, 15, 36, 62, 118,
    120
2.22 39, 42
2.23 39, 41, 45 n. 62
2.24 42
2.25 43, 46
2.29 45-46
2.32 49, 52, 58

3.1-12 15, 51
3.1-27 11
3.6 58
3.8 59
3.11 61, 170
3.13-27 15
3.18 63
3.22 64
3.24 10, 64
3.25-10 10

4.13 131, 135-37, 146, 152
4.14 132-35, 139 n. 184
4.14-21 12, 129
4.15 134-35
4.16 135-38
4.17 138, 141
4.18 139 n. 184, 142-44
4.19 141
4.20 130 n. 170, 140, 142-43, 144 n. 189
4.21 133, 140, 144-45
4.22-8.14 11, 69
4.23 77
4.24 134
4.26 78 n. 105, 88, 134
4.30 84

7.1-2 71
7.4 72, 75
7.5 72, 74
7.6 74, 75 n. 104
7.6-8 73
7.7 74-75, 81
7.8 75
7.9 76
7.9-12 75
7.10 78
7.11 79
7.12 80-81
7.13 81
7.16 65

8.1-14 69, 82
8.2 84, 92
8.3 85, 87-88
8.4 85, 87, 90, 99
8.5 86-87, 94 n. 123, 95, 98
8.6 88-89
8.7 88-89, 91 n. 119, 103
8.8 89, 99
8.9 90, 92
8.10 92-94
8.11 92, 94-95, 99
8.12 93, 95-96, 99
8.13 84, 100, 102
8.14 101-02

9.5-7 111
9.13 106
9.14 106, 120 n. 159
9.14-31 12, 105
9.15 107, 114, 160 n. 211
9.16 108, 113
9.16-21 109, 111, 113 n. 148
9.20 93 n. 120, 108 n. 140
9.21 109
9.22 110, 114 n. 151, 115
9.26 112
9.27 113 n. 149, 117
9.28 114-15, 117
9.29 115
9.30 117
9.42 65

General Index

10.2 12, 105, 119, 121
10.2-12 12, 105
10.3 121
10.5 123
10.7 125
10.13 65, 150, 158
10.16-35 12, 129, 147
10.17 150-51
10.19 152, 168
10.21-22 160
10.22 152
10.23 153
10.23-28 153
10.29 147, 153-54, 159, 166 n. 219
10.30 147, 155-56, 159
10.30-34 147, 155, 159
10.32 156, 159
10.33 157
10.34 148, 158-59, 160 n. 210
10.35 159

11.2 164, 170
11.3 165
11.5 163
11.6 165-67
11.7 166, 168
11.8 166
11.9-11 166
11.15 167-69
11.16 167-69
11.18 167, 169
11.19 169, 171 n. 224
11.21 168
11.24 169, 170-71, 171 n. 224
11.25 171
11.26 172
Aristophanes, *Frogs* 163 n. 214

Caesar 70, 74, 75, 81
Catullus 61 93 n.121
celibacy 14, 160-62, 165, 171; see also emasculation, sex
character, 3, 4 n. 12, 9, 38, 52, 59 n. 87, 65, 75 n. 104, 84, 87 n. 114, 105, 120, 122, 155, 166; see also actor
coitus 93
Coleman, K.M. 140
consilium 132
contaminatio 37
Cupid and Psyche 2 n. 4, 23 n. 32, 37-38 n. 57, 171 n. 227

decurion 109, 119, 125
Dionysian 89, 95, 151
Dionysus, see Liber / Dionysus, Aristophanes *Frogs*
discourse 1, 4-5
divorce 114, 126; see also marriage
dokimasia 50, 53, 67

Dowden, Ken 22 n. 29, 46 n. 65, 87, 89 n. 116
duumvir quinquennalis 147

ekphrasis 1
emasculation 36, 98, 103, 171; see also celibacy
Endymion 23
enemy 8, 74, 83, 96, 99, 100, 102; see also opponent
excursus 158, 160
exempla mythical, historical 158
exordium 56, 58

fellowship of Laughter 14, 52, 62, 68; - of Isis 14, 164, 170, 171 n. 224, 174, 175
festival of Laughter 11, 14, 15, 49-55, 57-58, 60-63, 65-68, 72, 164, 170, 171 n. 224, 173-75; *Risus* - 137 n. 180; - of *Ploiaphesia*, or Spring - 13, 163-66, 168, 172, 174
Finkelpearl, E.D. 51 n. 72, 57, 59 n. 86, 61 n. 90, 83 n. 112, 120, 121 n. 164, 137 n. 180, 148 n. 194, 149 n. 197, 159 n. 209
Freudian 47, 101
friend 8, 15-22, 24, 26, 27, 30-35, 54, 59 n. 87, 69, 84, 88, 90-91, 95, 111-12, 135, 137, 151; see also helper

Ganymedes 23
gender roles, reversal of 74, 83, 97
genre 2, 171 n. 227
Geryon 52, 58
Greimas, A.J. 2 n. 5, 3, 4 n. 9-12, 5 n. 14, 7 n. 15, 9; Greimasian 2, 4 n. 9, 5

Habinek, Thomas 51, 130 n. 170-71, 134 n. 178, 153 n. 200
haima 73
Helen 13, 148-49, 156, 158-59, 161
helper 3, 5-6, 8, 17, 22, 24, 33, 36, 41, 45, 47, 52-53, 74, 76, 78, 80, 85-86, 105- 06, 110, 114-15, 118, 122, 126, 131, 136, 140, 147, 154-55, 158, 166; see also friend
Homer *Odyssey* 95 n. 126, 156 n. 204, 168 n. 222; see also Odysseus, Ulysses

illness, 132, 165 n. 218; see also love-sickness
intersection of plans / schemes 8-10
intratextuality 31, 39, 40, 54, 60, 80, 84, 98, 111, 113, 118, 144
irony 83, 112, 116 n. 155, 121, 136, 139, 146, 153 n. 202, 158

General Index

Julio-Claudian 146
Juno 155-56, 158

Laughter, see festival of Laughter
Liber / Dionysus 84, 89
locus amoenus 31
love-sickness 121, 125; see also illness
lusus 61; see also festival of Laughter

marriage 12-14, 34, 36, 47, 66, 70, 82-84, 87-93, 96-97, 99, 100-03, 107, 148-49, 153-54, 155 n. 203, 156, 159-62, 171; see also divorce
McCreight, Thomas 24-25, 51 n. 71, 54 n. 76
miles amator 108
mimesis 154, 161
Minerva 155-56, 158
mirror, mirroring 2, 16, 34, 36, 47, 50, 54, 65, 67, 71, 82, 87, 91, 98-99, 106, 113-14, 117, 126, 141, 143, 148, 175
mise en abyme 21, 75
multiformity of Isis 2, 165
munerarius 131, 138, 152
munus 9, 129-32, 136-40, 143-44, 146-48, 151-52; see also spectacle
mystes 175

narratio 56, 58
narrative program 4-5; see also plan, plot, scheme
New Comedy, Greek and Roman 2, 38
noverca 4, 12, 105, 120, 124, 127

object / value 52, 110, 115
objectio ad bestias 13, 130-31, 140, 143, 147-48, 153-54
Odysseus 23-24 n. 32, 81 n. 111, 106, 119, 168; see also Homer *Odyssey*, Ulysses
opponent 3-4, 8, 22, 24, 27, 33, 41, 47, 52-53, 61, 74, 76, 78, 80, 83, 89-90, 92, 95, 98-99, 106, 110, 115, 122, 126, 131, 136, 140, 144, 147, 154-55, 159, 166-67, 173, 176; see also enemy
orator 50, 61, 72, 173
Ovid, *Amores* 108-09 n. 140

peroratio 56
Phaedra 119-20, 122, 127; see also *noverca*
pharmakos / scapegoat ritual 51, 55, 62, 153 n. 200
Philippides, S.N. 2 n. 5; 3 n. 6, 8; 4 n. 9-10, 12-13
plan 5, 8-11, 16-17, 21-22, 24, 26-27, 29-31, 33, 45, 47, 52-53,

69-70, 73-76, 78, 80, 83, 88-92, 98, 102, 105-07, 110-11, 113-16, 121-23, 126, 131-33, 140-42, 146, 176; see also plot, scheme, narrative program
Plato, *Phaedo* 170 n. 223; *Phaedrus* 31
Plautus, *Miles Gloriosus* 97; *Mercator* 97-98
Pliny, *NH* 171 n. 224
Ploiaphesia, see festival of
plot 2 n. 4, 4-5, 8-9, 16, 31, 50, 57, 59, 61, 66-68, 70-71, 73-76, 78-79, 81-83, 86, 98, 102-03, 107, 113, 117, 119, 126, 135-37, 140, 170, 171 n. 227; see also plan, scheme, narrative program
pompa, see procession
procession 44, 55, 60, 94 n. 124, 100 n. 130, 124, 164 n. 215, 166, 168
puer 111 n. 144, 114
pyrrhic 148, 154-55

receiver 3, 5, 22, 24, 53, 74, 76, 85, 110, 136, 140, 154-55, 166
Risus, see festival of Laughter
rite of passage 50, 53, 148-49, 154, 155 n. 203, 161, 171 n. 227; wedding / marriage / marital - 13, 70, 78 n. 105, 83, 88 n. 115, 93-94, 97, 101, 103, 148-49, 159, 161-62, 171 n. 225; integration - 51-54, 57, 61, 67-68; Isis - 1, 148, 161, 163, 169-70, 173; necromantic - 45, 47; funeral - 101; animal sacrificial - 25; Dionysian - 151
ritual, see rite
role-reversal, see gender roles

sacrifice 17, 24, 25, 30, 78-79, 87, 88 n. 115, 96 n. 127
satire 174
scaena 45, 89, 92, 107, 113 n. 149,
scheme 2, 5, 8-9, 12, 36, 44, 47-48, 69, 70, 75-76, 82-83, 85-86, 88, 92-95, 97-98, 101, 103, 107, 123 n. 166, 127, 130, 132, 135-37, 139-41, 146-47; see also plan, plot, narrative program
Schlam, C.C. 17 n. 20, 22; 31 n. 47; 36 n. 52; 37 n. 54; 53 n. 75; 63 n. 95; 94 n. 125; 106 n. 135; 121 n. 164; 124 n. 167; 149 n. 196; 151 n. 199; 157 n. 206; 158 n. 208; 166 n. 219; 171 n. 227

General Index

sea voyage 168, 170, 174
semiotic square 3, 9
sender 3, 5, 41, 53, 85, 122, 136, 140, 154-55, 165
Seneca, *Phaedra* 120
servitium 168
sex, sexual 12-13, 47-48, 64-66, 69, 83, 89, 96-97, 101, 107-08, 112-14, 123, 126, 148-50, 152-54, 156, 158-59, 160 n. 210, 161, 170; see also celibacy
Slater, N.W. 1, 130 n. 170
spectacle 1, 9, 12-13, 20, 38-39, 48, 81, 130 n. 170-71, 131-33, 135-37, 140-42, 145-49, 152-54, 161-62; see also *munus*
Spring festival, see festival of *Ploiaphesia*
subject 3-4, 8-9, 22, 24, 41, 45-46, 52-53, 74, 76, 85-86, 110, 115, 122, 136, 140, 154-55, 166
syntactical arrangement 3

Terence, *Eunuchus* 98, 152
theluphron 48
Trojan Horse 137, 141

Ulysses 23; see also Odysseus, Homer *Odyssey*

venatio 130, 140-41, 147
Venus 13, 23 n. 32, 64, 148-49, 155-59, 161, 171 n. 224
Vergil, *Aeneid* 2 51 n. 72, 136-37, 141; *Aeneid* 4 101 n. 132, 120, 121 n. 164; *Aeneid* 6 45 n. 64
voluptas 149, 156, 161-62, 170-71 n. 224

Wiedemann, T. 138 n. 183, 144, 147 n. 191, 148 n. 193
Winkler, J.J. 1 n. 3, 5 n. 14, 17 n. 22, 32 n. 49, 37-38 n. 56, 43, 44 n. 59, 46 n. 65, 60 n. 88, 62 n. 92, 78 n. 105, 106 n. 135, 107 n. 139, 116 n. 155, 153 n. 201, 160 n. 210, 171 n. 224, 174 n. 229

Zimmerman, M. 1, 120, 121 n. 164, 122 n. 165, 149 n. 197, 153 n. 201, 155 n. 203, 156 n. 205, 157 n. 206, 158 n. 207

GPSR Compliance

The European Union's (EU) General Product Safety Regulation (GPSR) is a set of rules that requires consumer products to be safe and our obligations to ensure this.

If you have any concerns about our products, you can contact us on ProductSafety@springernature.com

In case Publisher is established outside the EU, the EU authorized representative is:

Springer Nature Customer Service Center GmbH
Europaplatz 3
69115 Heidelberg, Germany

Batch number: 09747071

Printed by Printforce, the Netherlands